Joseph S. Lyles

Attorney at Law

How You Can Avoid Legal Land Mines

Book design: Nyoka Gray, Omni Graphics

First Edition editorial assistant: Kelly Hall

Editor, Second Edition: Wade Macfie

Cover Design, Second Edition: booksjustbooks.com

Manufactured in the United States of America

Printed by R. J. Communications, www.booksjustbooks.com

For information, write: Joseph S. Lyles
                           P.O. Box 17736
                           Greenville, SC 29606

Contents

Avoid Land Mines in Accident Cases   54

Real Estate   75

Final Words of Awareness   **129**

Appendices

Introduction

"Nobody . . . ever expected me to be President."
—Abraham Lincoln (1809-1865)

Few of us ever expect to have big legal problems. However, many of my clients found out the hard way that unexpected problems do happen. Many of their problems could have been avoided by simply taking some common-sense precautions, like reading contracts before signing them.

On the other hand, plenty of clients used their common sense, but lacked the basic understanding of the legal principles or laws that applied to their situations. Without that legal knowledge, they often walked right into legal minefields.

Another fertile source of people's legal problems is their belief in legal myths. Certain misunderstandings of the law are so widespread that they have become legal myths. Similarly, I have found that many legal rights that technically exist are, as a practical matter, almost impossible to enforce. Although you technically have the right to sue someone, as a practical matter it may be a waste of time.

This book offers real-life accounts of the more common or interesting mistakes by laymen that I have seen or experienced first-hand. Of course, this list is not exhaustive.

Take notes or use a highlighter while you read this book. Do whatever will help you learn this material, because it will help you avoid legal land mines. How? By reading this book, you will become sensitive to the situations and issues that often lead to legal trouble.

I also hope this book will provide readers with a new appreciation for what lawyers can do for their clients. Lawyers can play an important role in your life by helping you avoid legal snafu's, but you have to know when to ask for their help.

Last, do not act like the proverbial ostrich that sticks its head into a hole in the ground at the sight of danger. Be pro-active and preventive. No one can predict the future and the unexpected does happen — so prepare for it.

Acknowledgments

The leader of a team often gets credit for accomplishments that were actually made possible by a large number of team members. This is particularly true in the case of production of a book where the team has been an ad hoc group. Although the cover of this book says I am the author, in fact there are many who share its true authorship. Also, I have learned much of what I know about the law from various lawyers, judges and law partners with whom I've had the pleasure of dealing in the course of my law practice. Likewise, I owe a debt to my clients who allowed me to represent them and thus have the opportunity to learn about the practice of law "in the trenches".

In this edition I want to give special thanks to Wade Macfie who has served as editor, designer, computer software technician, and personal coach for me. Ongoing thanks also to Sherri Rosen of Sherri Rosen Publicity, who has both guided and pushed as was needed to keep the project on track.

Particular thanks go to Alex Sanders, a true Renaissance Man, for his leadership by example and his kind words.

Last, but certainly not least, I thank my family and many friends for their loving support.

CHAPTER 1

Strictly Legal (Or How to Swim With Sharks)

INTRODUCTION: CAN THEY SUE ME FOR THAT?

People are always asking me whether they can be sued for this, that or the other. There is rarely a short yes-or-no answer. Technically speaking, you can be sued for anything; the real issue is whether the party suing you will likely recover any damages.

Filing a lawsuit is relatively easy, but winning a lawsuit requires a lot of time, effort and money. And if someone does win an award of damages in a civil lawsuit, that alone does not guarantee the winner will ever collect from the loser.

Unless the loser of the lawsuit has insurance coverage that will pay the damage award, or equity in real estate to which the judgment can attach, then the loser may simply choose to ignore the judgment. The unpaid judgment may damage the loser's credit, but that may be a burden the loser is willing to bear. Some states allow judgment holders to garnish wages, but others, like South Carolina, do not allow such garnishment. Ultimately, the loser can always declare bankruptcy in an effort to avoid the judgement.

If you are sued for someone's personal injuries or property

damage and you have liability insurance coverage, notify the insurance company immediately. The company should provide an attorney to defend the lawsuit at no charge. However, if there is no coverage for the actions complained of in the lawsuit, you will have to hire an attorney to defend you or take the risk of representing yourself.

There are other checks and balances that discourage lawsuits. For example, an experienced attorney is not going to pursue an obviously frivolous lawsuit against you, especially if he or she is required to fund the lawsuit under a contingency fee arrangement. Also, the complaining party will be reluctant to pursue a lawsuit that the attorney advises is unlikely to succeed if the complaining party personally has to pay the attorney's fees and costs.

LESSON 1: KNOW WHEN YOU NEED A LAWYER

Getting legal advice is like getting preventive care on your car; if you do it now, you are less likely to have a big problem to fix later. Unfortunately, too many people try to solve their legal problems themselves and wait to seek professional help until the problem has become impossible to solve. Once you have signed a bad contract it is too late for an attorney easily to get you out of it. Once you have admitted your guilt to the authorities it may be too late to avoid a severe punishment. Once you sink money into a bad business deal, it is usually too late to obtain a full refund.

With the large number of lawyers practicing today, there is intense competition, which is good for consumers, because the competition holds down legal rates. Legal counsel can usually be obtained at a reasonable price, making it easy for people to get legal advice on any significant business deal, real estate transaction, or personal legal problem.

Because the volume of laws and regulations in our world is staggering, no lawyer attempts to know every one. Instead, good attorneys become skillful at finding law applicable to a particular situation. And with the Internet, even sole practitioners have equal access to research the law.

The Lesson: It is better to use attorneys to avoid problems than it is to use them to get you out of trouble. If you have doubts about whether or how to proceed in a situation that has legal ramifications, then be safe and consult an attorney. Why? An ounce of prevention really is worth a pound of cure.

LESSON 2: TIME LIMITS

Our legal system developed from the legal system of England which came across the Atlantic with the colonists from the British Isles. Much of the law was **case law** (also called common law) which was derived from written decisions of judges in case after case. One legal doctrine developed by the judges was called *laches*. This doctrine was based on the principle that someone should act within a reasonable period of time to exercise their legal rights. It is held unfair to let someone claiming to have suffered a legal wrong to wait many years before pressing a claim in the courts. The passage of time makes it more difficult for someone who has been sued to prepare and present a defense.

Now most time limits on filing legal claims are set forth in statutes, regulations or other written rules. Unfortunately, the time limits vary from law to law, state to state, civil to criminal law, contract to contract, etc.

Any right or remedy created by a legal rule or a law is going to be subject to time limitations.

For example, victims of sexual discrimination at work must complain to the appropriate government agency within a certain period of time or they will never be able to pursue a claim for damages against the perpetrator. Under some laws contracts are able to specify time limits for complaints or appeals. Yet other laws contain time limits that cannot be shortened by the terms of a contract. For example, the language of health benefit plans may prescribe limits for denial of claims, yet the language in automobile liability policies which attempts to shorten the time limit for filing lawsuits for the benefits is usually unenforceable.

The key to navigating around all these time limits is to be prompt in reporting any injuries or wrongs you suffer. For instance, if you are hurt on the job, be sure to report it to your supervisor as soon as possible. If there is a change of status that could affect your contract or statutory rights, report it to the cognizant authority as soon as possible. For example, if your 22-year-old child drops out of college and becomes ineligible for coverage under your health insurance policy, you must report that change to your company soon in order to preserve your rights to purchase an individual policy for him under the federal law known as COBRA.

Some time limits created by laws or regulations may help you. For example, there are time limits for health benefit plans to process your claims set by the Department of Labor regulations. The website of the appropriate governmental agency is a good place to look for time limits that may apply to your case (see Appendix G).

The Lesson: If an incident in your life seems to have potential legal implications, find out what the limits are on your ability to start remedial or protective action, and on the abilities of others to make claims against you.

LESSON 3: SAVE THAT PAPER!

When you or your lawyer are working to solve a legal problem there are two basic ingredients you need: first, you need the relevant facts; second, you need the relevant law. Your most important source for these ingredients is often paper, whether in the form of contracts, receipts, tax returns, accident reports, insurance policies or witness statements. Without these sources of information your and your attorney's efforts will be handicapped.

My advice here may directly conflict with that of the "organization expert" who encourages you to throw much of the paper in your life into the trash. To the contrary, I believe you should save as much meaningful paper as possible. My experience as a practicing attorney has taught me that documentary evidence is often the most important in any case.

This point is touched on in several of the lessons in this book. A piece of paper can be a hidden land mine in your case. If your attorney doesn't know about it and the other side does, a simple piece of paper can blow up in his face in court. and, of course, the reverse may be true to your benefit.

There are many reasons to keep papers. They can help you in ways not directly related to the law. For example, if you saved (and organized) all your receipts you could use them at the end of the year to see how you spent your money. Using this knowledge you could better plan your coming year's budget and identify areas to economize in. These same receipts could very likely be evidence in a divorce case or a tax case. And if you had a loss of property due to theft, fire or flood, those receipts would be valuable in establishing your insurance claim.

The Lesson: *From a legal point of view, it is better to have papers that you don't need than it is to need papers that you don't have.*

LESSON 4: DON'T IGNORE TRAFFIC TICKETS

Many people think that if they ignore a problem, it will just go away. That isn't the case with traffic tickets. In this era of computers, the government keeps track of traffic tickets efficiently and they don't just disappear.

When you ignore a traffic citation, the traffic court will try you in your absence, find you guilty of the offense and issue a warrant for failure to appear. One day you might be cruising down the road and get pulled over for a minor violation. The police officer will run a check on your driving record and discover the bench warrant, and you will be arrested and taken into custody.

Likewise, if you receive a letter from the state department of highways or public safety notifying you that your driver's license will be suspended, don't ignore it. Immediately contact a lawyer to request a hearing. If you can show the hearing officer a good reason to do so, the suspension may be lifted or avoided.

There is never a good time to be arrested and taken to jail. Even if you are released on bail, it will definitely ruin your day.

The Lesson: *Don't ignore traffic tickets or you will be setting yourself up for a legal land mine.*

LESSON 5: PROS AND CONS OF CASH TRANSACTIONS

Many people like to make transactions in cash. Cash is easy to use and, of course, easy to hide. It never bounces like a check, and it doesn't have to go through the banking system before you can have access to it. But the very aspect that makes it so attractive can be a drawback: it is difficult to document. If you pay cash for something and don't keep a receipt, you can have trouble proving the purchase.

For instance, if your income is primarily paid in cash, you can have difficulty proving loss of income in a personal injury claim. Likewise, if your spouse receives the bulk of his or her income in cash, you will find it almost impossible to prove that income in a family court case.

Obviously, many people who function primarily in a cash economy fail to claim the cash on their income tax returns. If they are involved in a court case and income is an issue, the other side will subpoena their tax returns. If they have not reported their income on their tax returns, they are going to find it almost impossible to establish a claim for loss of income, and their failure to pay taxes will be embarrassing, at the least.

Therefore, you need to be aware that with all the benefits of cash transactions, there are some drawbacks. You might say that cash is a double-edged sword; it cuts both ways. Its lack of a paper trail can be helpful or harmful.

The Lesson: *You need to be aware of the pitfalls of cash transactions and get written receipts when possible.*

LESSON 6: TALK TO YOUR LAWYER

Over the years, I've had many people contact me because they were mad at their lawyers. Usually, after investigating the situation, I found that the main problem was a lack of communication. I then recommended that the client and lawyer meet one-on-one and discuss the problem directly.

Too often, people seem to assume that their lawyers can magically divine the details of their cases, which, of course, they cannot. Telling your attorney *all* of the details of your case, and doing so *in person*, so that all the hints of body language and visual communication can contribute, is the best way to avoid confusion and misunderstanding.

For example, the legal system tends to move deliberately because the ultimate goal of our legal system is justice, not efficiency. But to clients this pace often seems extremely slow. In the absence of explanation from their lawyers, clients may assume that nothing is being done on their cases. In reality, the lawyer usually has done all he can do until the lawsuit is called for trial or until the other side of the case responds to some request. A simple conversation between the client and the lawyer about the delays and procedures would satisfy the client's concerns.

Don't be afraid to ask your attorney questions about your case. If you don't ask, the attorney will probably assume you don't want to know about some detail.

The Lesson: *You should meet with your lawyer before you decide to fire him or her. Usually clear communication will get the lawyer-client relationship back on track. Often problems can be avoided by keeping a notebook throughout the course of your case, bringing it to each meeting with your lawyer and recording the details of what is discussed and what your lawyer tells you about the case and its progress. This will eliminate the frustration of covering the same ground repeatedly and will provide a place to note the inevitable questions which will occur to you between meetings with your lawyer, ensuring that they will be on the table at your next session.*

CHAPTER **2**

The Business of Life

INTRODUCTION: PROTECT YOUR LIFESTYLE, HOME, AND SANITY

The old saying "trouble comes in threes" is often true. In fact, in the field of law, trouble seems to come by the dozen.

Over the years, I have been alarmed by how often someone who has one legal problem also has several other major problems in life, such as poor health, financial challenges, bad relationships or difficulties at work. These troubles can be the result of many different issues, but together they create one big minefield.

Most people are not defeated by one problem, but by a gaggle of festering troubles that can't be subdued. When a person is fighting many "battles" on many fronts, it is important for him or her to avoid legal problems. Unfortunately, however, just about every problem in a person's life has a legal component to it.

For example, if you are having a fight with your significant other, what does the law say about who gets what assets and liabilities if you split up? If your boss is extremely angry with you, what rights do you have to keep your job? If you have a disagreement with a dealer who sold you a car, what are your rights as a consumer? Or, if someone runs a stop sign and totals your car, what damages can you claim and what about your medical bills?

I've had more than one client involved in two separate car

accidents in the same day, neither of which was the client's fault. I've also counseled many clients who have separated from their spouses either right before or right after they were laid off from their jobs. And I've had plenty of clients whose significant others stole money from their bank accounts or created credit card debt in their names right before leaving relationships. This gives you an idea how quickly problems can multiply.

Is it fair? No, but these disasters do happen. So my advice is to be at least as careful in your personal life as you are in your business life. Be aware of the hidden land mines described in the stories in this chapter, so you can avoid a similar devastating predicament.

LESSON 7: BE CAREFUL WITH WHOM YOU LIVE

Regardless of your views on the morality of living with someone, there are legal land mines in your path if you live with someone without the legal status of marriage. The biggest problem with such a relationship is presented when it falls apart. Who gets what property when you split up? Will your partner be reasonable?

Jan lived with a man for about two years. During that time they opened a bar, and she worked in it without pay for a year. She helped renovate the building before the business even opened. When the business started running smoothly, Jan's significant other ended the relationship. That's when Jan found out how weak her legal position was as a live-in.

Jan did not have the title to the house where they lived, and her name was not on the lease of the building where the bar operated. She wasn't even listed as an owner on either title of the two vehicles they drove. Jan was unmarried and therefore could not file a divorce action and demand her fair share of the marital property. Without a marriage, there was no marital property to divide, and there was no paper trail to document her contributions to the business venture.

While there were some legal actions I, as Jan's lawyer, could take on her behalf, they were not as effective as a family court action.

The Lesson: If you really want to live with someone without the legal benefits of the institution of marriage, document who owns what and make sure to keep track of your contributions to any business ventures that you and your significant other start.

In addition, if you do not intend to be married and you live with someone, be careful not to create a common-law marriage. In South Carolina, for example, you become husband and wife by operation of the **common law** *(judge-made law, not statutory law) if you hold yourself out to the community as husband and wife. Contrary to popular opinion, the length of time you live together is not the deciding factor in a common-law marriage. The courts look at evidence, such as filing a joint tax return or signing a lease as husband and wife. The danger of common-law marriage is that one of the parties could be awarded both property and alimony in a divorce proceeding.*

LESSON 8: THE GAMES PEOPLE PLAY

If you have any friends or relatives, they will come to your residence sooner or later, or if you have children then undoubtedly their friends will come over to play. Statistically, you can be certain that at some point someone will be injured at your home. Many people have suffered injuries at the homes of others while engaged in a variety of activities, including swimming, partying, slipping and falling, riding motorized vehicles and playing.

Can guests sue you if they are injured while located at your home? Yes. Will they sue you? Maybe. Will they win? Maybe. Many factors will come into play, such as how badly they were hurt and how they were injured. Other factors include whether you were negligent in failing to warn them of the condition that caused the injury and whether there is healthcare insurance that will cover their bills.

The best way to protect yourself from having to pay a large amount of damages for someone else's injury on your property is to be well insured. You should have liability coverage with your homeowners coverage of at least one hundred thousand dollars, but more if you can procure it. You should also consider having umbrella coverage, which is coverage that applies once your liability limits have been paid out.

Probably the single most important insurance coverage to have is the no-fault type of coverage, which pays medical bills for anyone injured on your property, no matter the cause. It is often called

Medical Payments Coverage or Personal Injury Protection Coverage. This no-fault type of coverage is very valuable because it pays medical bills, which are usually the main component of damage claims. Someone could still pursue a judgment for pain and suffering, permanent impairment, or punitive damages even if their medical bills are paid, but he or she will be less likely to do so if those bills have been taken care of by your insurance.

In addition to being well-insured, you should be safety-conscious whenever you have visitors. If you have a dangerous situation on your property, you should post "No Trespassing" and "Danger" signs around it. Take photos to show that you placed such warning signs. Likewise, put up a fence around your swimming pool for safety's sake.

Finally, if someone is injured, be very attentive and offer your concern and sympathy. Treat them as you would like to be treated.

The Lesson: *Warn visitors of any hazards on your property and make sure your insurance policy will cover a visitor's injury.*

LESSON 9: DON'T CRY WOLF, BUT ALWAYS REPORT A CRIME THAT AFFECTS YOU

Bill's Case

Bill went to answer a knock at his door. When he opened it, he saw a police officer there.

"I have a warrant for your arrest," the officer said.

"What for?" asked Bill.

"For writing bad checks," came the reply.

Bill was stunned because he had never written a bad check, but he found himself on the brink of a legal minefield. Unfortunately, two years before, Bill's wallet was stolen from his car while it was parked in a rural area where he was swimming. He suspected a particular person, but he didn't bother to report the theft to the authorities.

As it turned out, the thieves had used Bill's ID to open a checking account. Then they proceeded to write bad checks using his driver's license. After the checks bounced, it took two years for Bill to be served the warrants because he lived in an adjoining county.

Bill could have languished in jail for a year or more while the government slowly prosecuted each bad check in a different Magistrate's Court. Fortunately, with the help of legal counsel, Bill was able to take care of all of them at once.

Over the years, I have also been consulted by several different women who were victims of sexual assault, generally unwanted touching or groping. One thing that they all had in common was the failure to report the assaults to the police. In addition, I've also talked with numerous female clients about physical abuse by their husbands. And again, very few had ever called the police at the time of the abuse.

Unfortunately for these women, there were rarely any witnesses to these physical or sexual assaults and batteries. Consequently, the civil cases that they wished me to pursue always boiled down to a swearing contest, and swearing contests are difficult to win.

The Lesson: You should always report a crime that affects you or someone else. If you are physically injured in any way, go to a doctor or emergency room right away so your injuries will be cared for and documented. Photograph any visible evidence of a crime, including bruises from physical attack. (If you may be a victim of abuse, see Appendix G for suggested resources).

LESSON 10: WHY HAVE A POWER OF ATTORNEY?

Having a close relative with a physical or mental disability can be challenging. With senior citizens, the biggest challenge can be determining when they have crossed the line between competence and incompetence. In other words, it is often difficult to know when they are no longer able to handle their affairs independently.

I've had clients with elderly relatives who managed to give away, spend, or lose large amounts of money before my clients realized those relatives suffered with mental disabilities. Of course, we don't want to hurt our beloved senior citizens' feelings by restricting their freedom unnecessarily. But, on the other hand, if you wait too long to put some safeguards in place, they can hurt themselves or others physically, emotionally or financially.

An older person who tends to be a little paranoid can suddenly take a very paranoid or unreasonable action, like trying to hide her money from everyone, giving mere acquaintances a power of attorney or refusing the help of a loved one. The best way to avoid these problems is to maintain regular contact with your relative and ask that he or she give you a **durable power of attorney**, which is a document that allows you to step in and take care of your relative's financial and legal affairs when the need arises. An attorney can prepare such an instrument and instruct you in its use.

Contrary to popular opinion, a power of attorney is useless once someone dies. This is because only a duly-appointed representative of an estate can take legal actions affecting the property of someone who has passed away. However, having a durable power of attorney can save a lot of time and money if a relative becomes incompetent. Without one someone will have to go to the Probate Court and get appointed Conservator and/or Guardian for the incapacitated person, which is a costly and paperwork-intensive process, especially if another relative contests these efforts.

Once you hold a power of attorney for an older relative or friend, you should stay in contact with that person and with his or her neighbors. It would also be wise to communicate with the manager of your relative's bank. Let him or her know to contact you if anything out of the ordinary happens, such as transactions made in the company of a stranger or the relative withdrawing unusually large amounts of money.

The Lesson: Once money has been withdrawn, it can disappear forever. And that money will probably be sorely missed because the elder may someday need medical care, some type of assisted-living arrangement, or nursing home care. You should obtain a durable power of attorney for any relative or friend you may be responsible for or whose mental or physical capacity you may be concerned about.

CHAPTER 3
The Business of Consuming

INTRODUCTION: HOW NOT TO CHOKE ON YOUR OWN FEAST

We are all consumers, whether we are rich or poor; young or old; bright or dim bulbs. Perhaps the one area of consumption that is universal to almost all Americans is transportation, particularly in the area of automobiles. Over the years I've received more phone calls from consumers complaining about something connected to autos than any other product. Consumers have problems with auto repairs, used autos, auto sales contracts, auto insurance, traffic tickets and auto accidents.

I have also had lots of legal dealings with consumers who have had problems with all aspects of retail purchases. People buy defective products, some of which cause them bodily injuries. Others fall at stores or have merchandise fall on them. People are charged with shoplifting and credit card and check fraud. Consumers have issues with warranties and service contracts.

Several decades ago there were few, if any, special laws that applied to consumer transactions. However, with the evolution of mass marketing in the later half of the twentieth century came a growing awareness that consumers needed more rights and remedies to counter the excessive bargaining power of the faceless corporations that manufacture and market consumer goods.

Today there are state and federal laws that protect consumers from unfair trade practices, deceptive advertising, monopoly abuses, unfair debt collection, unsafe products and other consumer hazards that once were allowed under the maxim of *caveat emptor*, or "let the buyer beware".

While most of us are aware of "lemon laws" that provide protections for purchasers of defective cars, you might be surprised to learn that there are similar laws for purchasers of sick pets in some states. Also, particular categories of consumers have received protection under special statutes. For instance, in some states farmers are protected by specific laws from the sale to them of contaminated seeds or defective pesticides. Similarly, consumers of so-called "organic" foods are protected by special labeling laws that regulate the use of terms like "natural", "whole food" or "organic".

Consumers must still be careful when they buy certain products. For example, buyers of used cars are not entitled to the same protections as buyers of new cars . Consumers who are injured by products made outside the country may find it hard to sue for their damages. And in all cases, oral promises are difficult to enforce.

It is important to save all documents related to purchases of consumer products. Instruction manuals, written warranties and written warnings or disclaimers can all be very important in litigation over defective products. For your part you should read and follow the safety instructions. Avoiding an injury is a much more satisfactory outcome than being compensated for one.

LESSON 11: HEALTH INSURANCE

As the cost of medical care and the cost of health insurance go up, consumers are taking a closer look at what they are getting for their money. Employers who once gladly offered health insurance benefits to the members of their workforces now find this benefit too costly. They reduce the benefits or make the employees pay a greater portion of the premiums or both. Yet medical care providers complain that the payments they receive from the health benefit plans come too slowly, in miserly amounts, and with too much red tape and bureaucratic interference with care decisions.

As a consumer you need to be aware of the unique legal nature of health insurance. The first aspect that is unique is that most people who think they are covered with health or medical insurance policies are not entitled to insurance benefits at all. Technically, they are covered by "health benefit plans" that are regulated by a Federal law (known as ERISA.), not by insurance policies *per se*. "So what?" You may ask. One of the biggest distinctions is that insurance is regulated at the state level, but health benefit plans are regulated at the Federal level. If you sue a health benefit plan for refusing to pay benefits you can not possibly get punitive damages; however, if you sue an insurance company for refusing to pay you insurance benefits you can ask for punitive damages.

Federal law gives a lot of discretion to the "Plan Administrator" in the making of decisions on the when, where and how much of paying benefits. In most cases brought under federal law against health benefit plans juries will not make decisions; instead a judge alone will decide the outcome of each case.

Another key difference in insurance policies and benefit plans is who ultimately pays your claim. In a benefit plan the company itself often pays part or all of the benefits; however, an insurance company ultimately pays under a health insurance policy.

Yet another important difference is that a health benefit plan is always created by a document which spells out the procedures for appealing denials of claims. You have to follow these procedures before you can file a lawsuit. However, in some states an insurance policy cannot validly require that you follow certain appeal procedures before you file a lawsuit claiming the company wrongfully refused to pay benefits.

The Lesson: Become familiar with the details of your medical coverage. If you are changing jobs, evaluate the coverage which is offered just as critically as you do the salary offered. Do not hestitate to re-file denied claims which you regard as legitimate. If your plan repeatedly denies a claim which you understand to be covered, seek the advice of an attorney.

LESSON 12: CONSUMER AND BUSINESS CONTRACTS DIFFER

A second lesson from Samuel's case in Lesson 61 below is that the law considers the signers of business contracts to be on equal standing from the point of view of their knowledge and sophistication. While that is often untrue, it is, nonetheless, the way the courts look at business contracts. On the other hand, if the contract is a consumer contract, one prepared by a business for use in a transaction with a consumer, then the courts look at it differently, usually with favor toward the consumer.

The law requires that consumer contracts be fair. For example, consumer contracts must have certain terms written in bolder, larger print, such as those relating to waivers of warranties and arbitration. And generally the courts look at the education and sophistication of the consumer, as well as the circumstances of the contract signing, to determine whether it is fair to hold the consumer to the terms of the contract.

In other words, the courts tend to uphold the fine print in business-to-business contracts, but not necessarily in business-to-consumer contracts. Also, state and federal statutes regulate the contents and form of consumer contracts, in an effort to make them fair.

Any businessperson who deals with consumer contracts should have all paperwork reviewed by an attorney with a good working knowledge of this area of the law. Even letters written to consumers to collect debts have to be written with certain language.

The Lesson: *Judges are more likely to try to save a consumer from contractual land mines, but are less likely to rescue business people from such traps for the unwary.*

LESSON 13: BUYER BEWARE! UNDERSTAND THE BASICS OF WARRANTIES

Fortunately, consumers are not solely dependent on makers of products to provide them with warranties for new items they purchase. All purchased goods come with one or more unwritten warranties called **implied warranties.**

There are two basic types of implied warranties: the **warranty of merchantability** and the **warranty of fitness for a purpose.** These warranties, or promises, exist by operation of law and are in addition to any written warranty that the manufacturer may provide. Such a written warranty is called an **express warranty.**

If a manufacturer wants to disclaim or deny the existence of a warranty, it must do so in bold-face type and must follow other specific legal requirements. However, a manufacturer cannot disclaim the implied warranty of merchantability.

Merchantability simply means that a product is what it purports to be. In other words, if it looks like a hammer and is sold as a hammer, it very well better be able to drive a nail. The warranty of merchantability seems obvious in the case of something simple like a hammer, but in the case of something complex, like a computer program, it is much more complicated.

The warranty of fitness for a purpose is a special case of a warranty of merchantability in which the customer is purchasing a particular product for a particular purpose, and the manufacturer or retailer is aware of that purpose. Under such circumstances the product is being sold with the implied promise that it will meet the purchaser's special needs.

The Lesson: If you have a problem with a defective product, don't assume you are limited to the written warranty. If you can't get the manufacturer or retailer to rectify the situation to your satisfaction, contact your state consumer protection agency or an attorney. If you are injured by a defective product you can use other legal theories to help in recovering damages. These theories include **negligence** *and* **strict liability** *in tort.*

CHAPTER 4
Sue The Bastards

INTRODUCTION: MAY I APPROACH THE BENCH?

The drama of the courtroom is often brought to us by the entertainment industry. Unfortunately, what the media shows is not what actually goes on during a real trial. The reality is typically very boring to everyone except the parties and their attorneys. Most trials are slow-moving compared to what is portrayed on television or in the movies. Real trials often involve somber witnesses who drone on laboriously about tedious details. However, if your money, property or freedom is at stake in a trial, you will not only be interested, you will likely be scared, intimidated or just plain confused.

The courthouse, like any unknown territory, is best visited with a guide. Courts have their own peculiar customs, unique rules, code words and dynamics. Not every trial is conducted in the same fashion, as customs and rules vary from place to place. You often need a lawyer to interpret these unusual conventions and help you stick to a safe trail.

Much of what is done and not done, said and not said, in a courtroom is the result of a centuries-old quest by people to achieve perfect justice. It has been a long and arduous journey from the decisions of Solomon to the current jury trial system.

The result is a system that strives to produce justice and succeeds most of the time.

The jury system has been around in one form or another since the Magna Carta was signed in 1215. However, in the United States its basic components have not varied since the U.S. Constitution was written. Nonetheless, small changes are made from time to time to "fine tune" the system. A good trial lawyer knows these changes and how best to incorporate them into the trials of cases.

As communications technology changes, its new forms are slowly allowed into the courtroom. Judges typically are cautious in allowing the use of new technology in their courtrooms. Thus, if you want to use cutting edge technology in proving your case, you should get an attorney who knows what the judges will and will not allow.

Read on for further advice on braving the jungles of the courtroom. Armed with knowledge and guided by an attorney, you can travel this road in safety on your journey for justice.

LESSON 14: DON'T REPRESENT YOURSELF IN COURT

"A man who has himself for a lawyer, has a fool for a client."

—Abraham Lincoln

The primary reason you should not act as your own lawyer is that it is very hard to be your own advocate while maintaining credibility. A lawyer is first and foremost an advocate for his or her client's best interest. Yet, it is hard to argue strongly one's own position in a dispute. You will be less likely to push your own position as effectively as an attorney would.

The courtroom is a unique environment with its own unique set of rules. While many of these rules of procedure are based on traditions that are hundreds of years old, other rules are the result of recent enactments or judicial orders. Thus, you must follow a complex, evolving set of rules if you are acting as a lawyer in a courtroom. In addition, you need to be aware that jury trials proceed in a certain order. You must know and be able to apply properly in their legal context such terms as "objection," "sustained," "denied," "admission," and "evidence". These technical terms and the controlling rules of evidence are like land mines to the layperson who attempts to try his or her own case in court.

Properly trying a case in court is not easy. It is stressful and demanding, and it requires enormous concentration, alertness and well-orchestrated efforts. For these reasons, and others, few attorneys actually like to try cases, and the vast majority of attorneys stay away from the courtroom. Jury trials are particularly demanding and are even more carefully avoided by most attorneys than judge-alone or bench trials.

Ben's Case

I represented a couple who agreed to purchase a lot from a man named Ben. They intended to place a manufactured home on the land. Unfortunately Ben, the seller, had not used an attorney to prepare the contract of sale, but instead simply used a form contract. This form contract was intended for a sale that involved the buyer paying the entire purchase price at one time at the "closing." However, Ben had knowingly agreed to owner-finance the sale, thus allowing the buyers to pay in installments over several years.

The form contract Ben used also provided that the county property taxes on the lot be paid by the seller until closing. Because the sale of the land was not complete until the final installment was paid, the closing could not occur until then. As a result, Ben was required to pay the property taxes on the land for several years, which is normally the responsibility of the buyers. A simple meeting with an attorney would have saved Ben thousands of dollars.

The Lesson: The legal profession, like medicine, is one that should not be attempted by amateurs.

LESSON 15: REMEMBER THAT LAWS VARY WITH LOCALITY.

Jeff, a man living in my home state of South Carolina, was licensed to practice law in New York. That was impressive because the New York bar exam has the reputation of being the most difficult in the country. Jeff, however, was not licensed to practice in South Carolina, which meant he might not have been aware of many South Carolina laws.

Jeff worked for a textile company and did not practice law, but he prepared his own Last Will and Testament. I'm sure he did an excellent job under the law of New York, but unfortunately, the law of South Carolina applied and was unique in that it required that a Will be witnessed by three witnesses, not two as is required in most states, including New York. (This unusual requirement has since been abolished, and South Carolina has joined the rest of the nation in only requiring two witnesses).

 The outcome was that Jeff's widow found his Will was worthless in the South Carolina Probate Court. Jeff's failure to look into the laws of the state in which he was living cost his wife a lot of money and led to the estate property passing to beneficiaries named in the intestacy statute, instead of those he named in his Will.

The Lesson: Be keenly aware that the law varies from state to state in many aspects. Be sure you are following the proper state's law when you are writing or interpreting any important legal document or making a contract.

LESSON 16: KNOW THE DIFFERENCE BETWEEN BEING RIGHT AND PROVING YOU ARE RIGHT IN COURT.

The public image of the legal system and its reality are not the same. Over the years, television and movies have successfully entertained the public with legal dramas. Using actors, not lawyers, the producers of these legal dramas are able to make trials seem action-packed, realistic and captivating. However, real trials are rarely exciting and often seem to move at a snail's pace.

For the sake of telling interesting stories, writers of legal shows have to make the issues clear. The cases are reduced to the bare essentials so the basic story can be presented quickly and concisely to the audience. An actor is not really trying to persuade a judge or jury, he is trying to entertain an audience. On the other hand, in a real jury trial, it is usually necessary to go into a great amount of detail because it is difficult to predict what facts are going to be important to jurors or judges. The issues are often confusing.

Another common misconception created by scripted legal shows is that the truth always comes out in court. The reality is that what actually comes out in court may be only partial truth. The Rules of Evidence and other policies often prevent a jury from hearing or seeing all the possible evidence. Ultimately, the jury has to make a determination based on an incomplete picture.

In our system of justice, the goal is perfect justice, but perfection is rarely reached. Any system dependent upon human judgment, like our legal system, is subject to errors. It is important to understand that in real life, the guilty party rarely erupts with a spontaneous confession in the courtroom as in the movies or television shows.

Be very cautious about assuming you know what a trial is really like. You may find that your knowledge is actually based on what you've seen on TV or the big screen, or read in a book.

The Lesson: *If you want to know how a real trial is conducted, you need to observe one. Admission is free, and it is very educational. If you have a case pending, or are considering filing one, don't let your own trial be the first one you've ever observed. Refer to APPENDIX C for more information on how to win a legal case.*

LESSON 17: DO NOT GIVE STATEMENTS

A common mistake people make is giving a recorded or written statement to an insurance adjuster or law enforcement officer. Both types of statement-takers are only concerned about their own interests. In other words, they are trying to further the goals of their employers, not help you, no matter how nice they act.

I've had clients over the years who agreed to give statements before they were represented. For example, in a personal injury case, a client might say something such as, "it was just an accident," without realizing that this statement could destroy the possibility of recovering damages for negligence. You must remember that words often have different meanings in the law than they do in everyday conversation.

No matter how sincere your explanation for a situation may be, you may find that you are nonetheless guilty of violating some law. Whenever you are asked to give a statement that has potential legal consequences, you should decline until you fully understand what kind of trouble you could get in.

The Lesson: *Never agree to give a statement without first consulting an attorney.*

LESSON 18: THE DIFFERENT STANDARDS OF PROOF IN CIVIL AND CRIMINAL COURT

One good effect of the O. J. Simpson trials is that they clearly demonstrated the difference between a criminal prosecution case and a civil damages case. The first O. J. trial was a criminal prosecution, and the second trial was a civil damages case. And while the verdicts may have seemed inconsistent, they actually were not so in a technical legal sense.

The key question the jury was answering in the criminal case was whether the government had proven that O. J. was guilty beyond a reasonable doubt. However, in the civil case the key question the jury was answering was whether the plaintiffs (the Brown family members) had proven by the greater weight of the evidence that O. J. wrongfully caused his wife's death.

The end results of criminal and civil trials differ. If O. J. had lost the criminal case, he would have been punished. His punishment could have included imprisonment and a monetary fine, and the sentence could have been suspended for a period of probation. A condition of probation can be monetary restitution. In some states he could have also been subject to capital punishment. Because O. J. was found liable (not the same as guilty) to the plaintiffs in the civil case, he was obligated only to pay money damages.

The main point the different verdicts highlight is that criminal cases and civil cases have different burdens of proof. In both cases, the prosecution or plaintiff has the burden of proof. But the burden is heavier in a criminal case because someone's liberty is at stake. In short, in a civil case, the side that is simply more believable wins, but in a criminal case, the jury must believe in the accused's guilt beyond a reasonable doubt.

Another big difference between criminal and civil cases is the way the decision of the court or jury is ultimately enforced. In a criminal case, the police often apprehend a convicted defendant in the courtroom and haul him off to jail. In a civil action, the victorious party is simply handed a piece of paper called a judgment. The police do not arrest the defendants if they refuse to pay the plaintiff the amount of the judgment.

I was involved with a case that illustrates how the different standards of proof can have a big impact on how a case is handled. My client, John, owned a raft rental company. One night while John was in his residence beside his business, a trespasser came onto his property and cut up two of his rafts with a knife. The rafts were fully inflated on the lawn in front of the store, awaiting customers who had reserved them for the following morning.

John barely glimpsed the perpetrator as he drove off in a brand new pickup, but he did see the yellow paper tag on the back of the truck. The tag proclaimed the name of the dealership that had recently sold the truck.

John called the sheriff who sent a deputy to investigate. They gathered evidence pointing in the direction of a man that John knew was not his friend. However, the local prosecutor refused to take the case because he didn't feel he could prove it beyond a reasonable doubt.

However, I successfully pursued a civil suit for John, and he won a verdict for monetary damages. Because the perpetrator owned real estate, we were able to actually collect the judgment, but the perpetrator never received any criminal punishment for his wrongdoing.

The Lesson: It is important to understand whether a particular case is classified as criminal or civil. This fundamental distinction controls how the case will be tried and concluded. The winners and losers in these fundamentally different types of cases have different burdens of proof and different obligations. And as O. J. Simpson's cases show, that distinction can be vitally important to the outcome of the case.

LESSON 19: WHO MAKES THE DECISION?

One of the frustrating aspects of the law is that it isn't always black or white. More often than not it's gray, in lots of shades. So a lawyer can rarely give a short answer to the question, "Is it legal?"

Under our system of law, there are two primary sources of law: **statutes** and **case law**. Ours is what is known as a **common-law** system of justice. Common law is law that is derived from written reports of previous cases, while statutory or code law is that taken directly from laws enacted by a legislature. However, even statutes have to be interpreted and applied to a particular case so the common-law approach is still used in cases involving statutory law.

Case law is sometimes called judge-made law. Under the common-law approach, a judge reads cases she thinks involve facts similar to the case at hand. The general rules or doctrines that these case decisions follow are then applied to the case before the judge. This common-law approach, of course, gives a judge leeway to rule on the case as she sees fit. Although the judge should follow the precedent established in the earlier case, there is plenty of room for interpretation.

The decision of a case is normally a two-step process. First, the judge determines exactly what the relevant facts are of the case. Then, the judge applies the law, as he interprets it, to the facts and produces a decision.

The problem faced by lawyers is that two judges deciding the same exact case can come up with two different decisions. And because no two cases are really ever exactly the same, it can be impossible to predict how a case will ultimately be decided. Thus, knowing the specific judge who will decide your case may be helpful.

That brings us to the topic of forum. **Forum** means what court will decide a case. Every court has different amounts of authority (**jurisdiction**) and different procedural rules. There are two basic courts: **trial courts** and **appellate** (appeals) **courts**. It can be very confusing because the same judge can be acting as a trial judge one day and an appellate judge the next day. In many states, the trial courts, listed in approximate order from lowest jurisdiction to highest jurisdiction are:

- Municipal Court (City Court): Includes criminal jurisdiction, primarily traffic and other minor criminal offenses.

- Magistrate's Court (Summary Court or Small Claims Court): Includes civil and criminal jurisdiction, but amounts in dispute are limited as are punishments for crimes.

- Family Court: Includes jurisdiction limited to family related cases, such as divorce and child custody.

- Probate Court: **Probate** of wills and estates, conservatorships, guardianships and commitments.

- Circuit Court (State): Includes civil and criminal jurisdictions.

- District Court (Federal): Includes civil and criminal jurisdictions.

In addition, there are several special federal courts with limited, specific jurisdictions, such as Admiralty, Tax and Military Courts.

All states have a variety of courts with different types and scopes of jurisdiction. If you are involved in a lawsuit or are considering filing one, it is important to know the limits of jurisdiction of the court that will handle the suit.

South Carolina and other states also have a type of judge called a hearing officer, who is a judge who rules on cases directly involving administrative agencies such as the State Alcohol and Beverage Commission or the Workers Compensation Commission. At the federal level we find hearing officers as well, such as Social Security Judges.

I know at some point while reading this book you will want to throw up your hands and yell, "Why does it have to be so complicated!" The reason our legal system is so complicated is that people are complex beings who live in complex societies and use complex technology. In many ways our laws mirror our society.

The Lesson: If you understand the basics of the legal system, it will seem less complicated. And knowing which court (forum) you want to be in will give you a head start in solving legal problems that could result in a lawsuit. If you have the opportunity to pick your forum, please get the advice of an experienced trial attorney. Different courts are suited for different kinds of cases.

LESSON 20: JUDGES ARE POWERFUL, BUT...

When couples divorce, the family court judge often makes one side or the other responsible for paying a particular debt, like a car or house payment. The person who is not ordered to make those payments will often assume that the judge's order gets them completely off the hook, but it doesn't.

A family court judge does not have the authority to alter an existing contract between a third party, like a creditor bank, and the couple who have come before him for a divorce. The creditor is still free to enforce its contract with either party, or both, assuming they both signed the original loan documents. In other words, your creditors can still sue you on a debt even if a judge ordered your spouse to pay the debt.

The power of any court to affect an existing contract is limited to interpreting it, not changing it. While one side or the other to a contract may feel a court's interpretation of a contract changes it, the court is supposed to enforce only the contract as the parties understood it at the time it was made.

Courts also find implied agreements in written contracts. The most common implied agreement is the **covenant of good faith**. This legal fabrication was created by judges who saw that a strict, technical interpretation of a contract's terms could cause unfair results to one side or the other. To avoid what they saw as unfair results, particularly in insurance contracts, the judges decided that there is an implied agreement among all parties to a contract that each side will act in good faith while following the contract.

The Lesson: Never assume a judge will save you from a bad contract you have entered, nor will a Family Court judge extinguish a debt you created while married. It's important for you to consider carefully the terms of any contract you are signing, because you are probably going to have to live with those terms. Unless the contract is very simple, it would be wise to have an attorney review it to avoid land mines lurking in the language.

LESSON 21: ALTERNATIVES TO YOUR DAY IN COURT: MEDIATION AND ARBITRATION

Mediation and **arbitration** are two ways of resolving legal cases that are alternatives to jury trials. They are known as **Alternative Dispute Resolution** (ADR), and they are becoming increasingly popular. Some jurisdictions are requiring that cases be mediated before they are tried, and some contracts require that disputes be resolved by arbitration because the authors of the contracts prefer arbitration to jury trials.

Mediation is a structured settlement conference usually conducted at an attorney's office. All sides to a dispute are present, often with their attorneys. A neutral, unbiased person (usually an attorney) is present to act as the mediator, and the choice of that person to act as the mediator is either agreed to by the parties or made by a court. The mediator must have had experience or training, or both, that provides the skills for getting opposing sides to reach a compromise. However, the mediator does not decide the case. If it is not settled, the case eventually proceeds to trial.

Mediation is scheduled at a time and place agreeable to all parties involved. Procedurally it is informal, unlike a trial in a courtroom. The conversation between the parties during the mediation is usually confidential and cannot be used in court.

Arbitration, on the other hand, involves the use of one or more people called arbitrators to reach a decision in the case. There are two basic kinds of arbitration: binding and non-binding. In binding arbitration, the arbitrator's decision is the final decision and there is no trial of the case. Usually the case is then ended with the parties following the decision of the arbitrator, although it is possible for a party to appeal the arbitrator's decision to a court.

In non-binding arbitration, the decision of the arbitrator is simply advisory. The parties may choose to disregard the decision. The main purpose of non-binding arbitration is to provide the parties with strong guidance from a neutral, unbiased third party. It gives them the opportunity to see how a judge or jury would likely rule on their case. Once they have the arbitration decision they are likely to settle the case.

There is a growing trend for parties to written contracts to agree to have any disputes arising from those contracts decided by arbitration. The courts uphold these clauses, even when one party did not read the arbitration clause in the contract. The general policy of our courts is that alternative dispute resolution (ADR) should be encouraged. The court system is seen as overburdened and, thus, too inefficient to deal with all the cases being filed. Therefore, if a judge can take a case off his list of cases to try (called a **jury roster**) by finding that it should be submitted to arbitration, then that is what he will probably do.

I have found in my legal practice that ADR is usually superior to a jury trial as a means of resolving disputes, because in ADR the costs are usually lower; the scheduling is much more convenient; and the proceedings are much less stressful. More importantly, the results are often more reasonable than the results of jury trials.

The outcome of a jury trial is always unpredictable. No one knows what a jury is going to do in any one case. Of course, if people did know how juries were going to rule on their cases, the winners would have no reason to agree to compromise beforehand. Mediation allows you to avoid the uncertainty of a jury trial.

Mediation offers the additional advantage of allowing the parties to fashion a unique solution to their problem. Oftentimes the parties in a mediation can fashion a compromise agreement that involves specific remedies that are not available to a jury. Thus, the settlement can be crafted to meet the unique needs of the parties. In fact, in a dispute between former business partners, there may be other possessions or rights one can give to the other side besides money. Equipment, customer lists, products, endorsements, real estate or future receivables might be given to one party by another party as part of the settlement. But, in a civil jury trial, the jury can only award monetary damages.

Moreover, I find mediation a helpful way to get a case settled because it forces all those concerned to get together and focus on the case, and nothing but the case. By meeting in a neutral location, the parties involved get away from distractions and the influences of the "home field". And by focusing on only one case, they are able to arrive at an understanding of how it should be settled. Also, having the mediator there to discuss the case helps put it in perspective. Each party is better able to understand the weaknesses of its case.

I'm sure there are a few cases that should be decided by a jury; however, for the vast majority of cases I have handled, I would have preferred a settlement through mediation or a decision through arbitration.

Although our system of justice is built upon the premise that a jury is the best decision-maker, the reality is that some juries base their decisions on irrelevant details, prejudices, and misunderstandings. Thus, most attorneys want juries to decide their cases only if all possibilities for settlement have failed.

With jurors you have limited information about who they are, but with arbitrators you generally are well acquainted with their history and credentials. And with mediation, you don't have to worry because the mediator will not make the decision, you will.

A case that would take at least a day to try before a jury can be presented to an arbitrator in two hours or less. Although mediations generally take longer than arbitrations, they are faster and usually much less stressful than jury trials.

In addition, arbitrations and mediations are less stressful because they allow disputing parties to retain a tremendous amount of control over their cases; while in a jury trial the parties turn over control of much of the case to a judge. Of course judges try to be fair, but they are sometimes concerned only with processing cases according to their own timetable. In those cases, the scheduling needs of the disputing parties are given little, if any, consideration.

The Lesson: Be sure to discuss ADR with your attorney early in your case. If you are given the choice of submitting your case to ADR, opt for it instead of a jury trial, unless your attorney explains that a trial would be a better choice.

LESSON 22: BEWARE OF LEGAL MYTHS ABOUT EMPLOYMENT LAW.

One of the legal myths I hear often is that an employer can't fire an employee without a good reason. The sad truth is that in a "right to work" state like South Carolina, you can be fired for any reason or no reason, as long as the firing doesn't violate a constitutional or statutory right; you cannot be fired because of your race, disability, age, sex or religion. And there are a few other statutory limitations, such as prohibitions against firing you for serving on a jury or for making a workers' compensation claim (referred to as a **retaliatory discharge**). If you have a written employment contract, handbook or policy manual, it may give you other protections from being fired. But other than those exceptions, your employer doesn't even have to give a reason for firing you. It may not seem fair, but there is no legal requirement that an employer be fair, only that he act constitutionally.

An employer can fire you because your tongue is pierced or you took too long on a smoke break. Your employer can fire you for being late to work, and for just about any other reason. Under the national laws governing family leave and disabilities, there are additional restrictions, but not all employers come within the restrictions of those laws. Also, government employees have certain rights to various hearings and reviews before they can be fired.

There are also federal and state statutes that provide protections for "whistle blowers" or people who report fraud perpetrated against the government by their employers. In addition, your employee handbook may give you rights to certain procedures before you can be fired.

If you suspect you are going to be fired unfairly, try to legally obtain copies of your personnel file. And if you are fired, request that a written explanation for your dismissal be provided in addition to any oral explanation. Then you will have some evidence for your attorney to review and advise you based upon these items of evidence. Written documents are much more helpful to your attorney than reports of rumors, suspicions and innuendo.

The Lesson: Because there are more and more laws applying to the employer-employee relationship, you should consult an attorney about any serious problem you have with your employer or employee. However, beware of legal myths, such as that an employer has to have a good reason to fire you.

LESSON 23: UNDERSTAND THE LIMITATIONS OF BANKRUPTCY

Beth struggled to keep a small business going after she and her husband, who was also her business partner, separated. With so many problems to deal with, Beth was distracted and wrote some checks that bounced.

Because she was overwhelmed and broke, Beth represented herself in the Federal Bankruptcy Court when her business failure and marital problems left her few, if any, alternatives.

If you properly prove your case, the Bankruptcy Court will relieve you of the legal responsibility to pay your debts. The order from the Bankruptcy Court that awards you this relief is called a **discharge**.

Beth had learned enough from researching on the Internet to successfully receive a discharge of her personal and business debts from the Bankruptcy Court. However, Beth failed to grasp one critical distinction: a bankruptcy discharge only protects a person from civil liability for his or her debts; it does nothing to insulate that person from criminal liability.

Subsequently, a merchant who received one of the bad checks tried to prosecute her. Ultimately, the merchant agreed to drop the prosecution, but Beth could have been convicted and punished.

If you write a bad check on a personal banking account, you may be a law-breaker, and bankruptcy does not protect you from criminal prosecution.

Filing bankruptcy also does not simply erase all your debts. Depending on many factors, you may have to give up your house, car, or other property if you file bankruptcy. In addition, as you probably already know, filing bankruptcy hurts your credit rating. You may find it very hard to obtain a traditional loan or credit card for years after filing bankruptcy.

Finally, bankruptcy laws are subject to change by Congress. Those changes could make filing for bankruptcy less attractive to debtors. Therefore, before filing a petition for bankruptcy, make sure you discuss your situation with an experienced bankruptcy attorney to avoid creating unnecessary problems.

The Lesson: Bankruptcy isn't a cure-all; it has pros and cons that need to be carefully considered before filing.

CHAPTER **5**

Avoid Land Mines in Accident Cases

INTRODUCTION: DON'T GET INJURED BY THE SYSTEM WHEN YOU HAVE AN ACCIDENT

So-called "accidents" are commonplace, dangerous and expensive in our present-day world. With the heavy use of technology, we are called upon to have good judgment, good reflexes and good luck when we are driving, working or playing at speeds far in excess of the pace of life at which our ancestors were required to live. Modern machinery not only multiplies the speeds but also the forces we deal with. Thus, the personal injuries that can result from automobile collisions or industrial accidents are often horrendous.

The aspect of our law that deals with the compensation of victims of personal injuries is often called the **tort** system. On-the-job injuries are usually dealt with by a statutory scheme called the **workers' compensation** system. Because the injuries sustained by the victims of accidents can be very costly in terms of medical expenses, rehabilitation expenses and lost income, the stakes in a tort case can be very high. And because there are so many companies and individuals that can be affected by the outcome of a tort case, the system is plagued with traps for the unwary.

You need to understand the basics of a tort case and what pitfalls should be avoided. What you do and say immediately before and after an accident can have a big impact on who wins, who loses and how much is won or lost in the resulting legal case. Read on as I lead you through this special minefield.

LESSON 24: IF YOU NEED A DOCTOR, GO TO A DOCTOR, NOT A LAWYER

I have seen several automobile accident cases in which the injured person went to a lawyer before seeking medical attention, and I understand why. The victims are concerned about having to deal with huge insurance companies without knowing their rights, and they are worried about creating medical bills that might not be covered by any insurance. They are wise enough to realize that what they do early on in the process can adversely affect the outcome, but there is a problem with this approach.

Anyone making a claim for personal injuries received in a car accident may be faced with a huge wall of skepticism. It will seem that almost everyone involved with documenting your auto accident and providing your medical care is treating you as if you had wanted it to happen. They will suspect you are trying to get something for nothing.

It is unfortunate, but the public in general and insurance companies in particular don't trust people when they say they were injured in a car wreck unless they have broken bones or bleeding cuts. And, because soft-tissue injuries don't show up on x-rays, they may question their existence. Unfortunately, only those who have suffered a soft-tissue injury from an accident understand that the pain and loss of mobility are very real.

Therefore, to avoid creating skepticism towards an injury claim, after an accident see either an emergency room physician or a family doctor as soon as possible. Don't go to your attorney until after at least one visit to a doctor.

The Lesson: *Get the facts about your case, including a doctor's diagnosis of your injury, and then consult an attorney; however, don't give a statement to an insurance adjuster before you consult an attorney.*

LESSON 25: TELL YOUR DOCTOR ALL YOUR MEDICAL COMPLAINTS

People who have been injured in an accident sometimes fail to mention all their problems to their doctor. For example, it is common for someone whose neck or back was injured in a collision also to have headaches and insomnia. If the injured person mentions neck or back problems, but fails to mention the other problems, then the doctor surely won't document those other complaints in his or her records. Later when the insurance company adjuster is reviewing the claim, he will not consider the headaches or insomnia because there is no reference to them in the medical records.

As far as insurance adjusters are concerned, if it is not written in the medical records, it didn't happen. And if it didn't happen, you will not be compensated for it by the insurance company.

The Lesson: Your failure to mention all your injuries to your doctor will prevent you from being adequately compensated for those injuries.

LESSON 26: WORKERS' COMPENSATION

If an employee is injured while working, then under most circumstances he or she is entitled to compensation in one or more of three ways:

1. Medical treatment
2. Wage replacement and/or
3. Monetary award for permanent injury.

However, there are limitations to all of these benefits. For example, your employer has the right to control and direct your medical treatment. Therefore, you may be directed to go to the company doctor. Some smaller companies do not have specific company doctors and will allow you to choose your own.

Wage replacement varies from state to state, but it essentially consists of a percentage of your wage that is paid to you once you have been unable to work for a period of time due to your injury.

The monetary award you are entitled to for your permanent injury, if you have one, is based on the number a doctor assigns as your **permanent impairment rating.** The higher your wage rate and the higher your impairment rating, the higher the amount of money you should be awarded. An attorney can help ensure you are properly compensated.

However, under workers' compensation law, you may not obtain damages for pain and suffering or punitive damages from your employer for an on-the-job injury. You may, though, still have a third-party claim against someone who wrongfully injured you. For example, the manufacturer of a defective machine that injures you on the job may be held liable to you in a civil action for actual and punitive damages. You will need an attorney to pursue this type of claim. Also, be aware that there are special time limits for filing for workers' compensation. Always report an injury to your supervisor as soon as possible.

The Lesson: Know what benefits you are entitled to when you are injured at work. Also, inform your supervisor immediately if you are injured on the job.

LESSON 27: HASTE MAKES WASTE, SO DON'T RUSH TO SETTLE A PERSONAL INJURY CLAIM

In the case of an auto accident or similar personal injury case, you should not be in too much of a hurry to settle your case. All auto accident claims are segregated into two parts: the property damage claim and the bodily injury claim. The insurance company for the wrongful party (the at-fault driver) should handle your property damage claim relatively quickly after the wreck, but there is no reason to hurry with your bodily injury claim settlement. If you have been injured in a car wreck, don't settle your bodily injury claim before enough time has passed for you to determine the full nature and extent of your injuries.

An insurance adjuster may approach you shortly after your collision and offer you about $500 to settle your injury claim. Don't take it! Even if you don't think you're hurt, wait a few weeks to make sure. And if you have been hurt, wait until after your doctors have finished treating you before you even consider settling your case.

The only time limit you need to be concerned about is the Statute of Limitations. The Statute of Limitations is simply a state or federal law that sets a limit on how long you have to file a lawsuit after an injury. In South Carolina, the limitation period is three years to sue an individual or corporation, and two years to sue any state agency or governmental entity. However, if you were injured on a ship or railroad or by a federal government employee or agency, a special federal statute may apply.

If you were injured a year or more ago, you should be concerned about the statute of limitations period, and contact an attorney. Find out exactly how long you can wait before your injury claim would be barred or prevented. Thus, you should not be in a big hurry to settle an injury claim, but you should also not wait too long to file a lawsuit. Once your lawsuit is filed, the statute of limitation is no longer a concern.

> **Note:** Also, be aware that employment discrimination claims have certain shorter time limits. If you think you were a victim of illegal employment discrimination, you should report it at once to the Equal Employment Opportunity Agency office nearest you.

Another reason you should avoid settling your personal injury claim too early is that doctors generally begin treatment conservatively. In other words, doctors often don't even consider surgery unless your injury is patently obvious, like a broken bone or bad laceration, and they sometimes delay running expensive tests, like an MRI*, until they have given your injury some time to heal on its own.

Often doctors assume back and neck injuries are mere sprains and strains. That assumption holds until the pain caused by the injury refuses to respond to anti-inflammatory medications, physical therapy and the passage of time. Then if the pain doesn't greatly improve, doctors start suspecting more serious injuries like herniated discs. Consequently, your doctor may not even send you for an MRI* until you have been hurting for several months.

If you settled your claim after two months and you later learned you had a herniated disc that needed surgery, then you would have to pay for the surgery with your own resources. You could not open the claim again. Taking time to assess your injuries can ensure that you are appropriately compensated and that you have enough money to pay for all the medical care you need.

The Lesson: Do not settle your injury claim until you are fairly certain that the full extent of your injuries is known. But do not wait so long that you are in danger of going beyond the Statute of Limitations. A good rule of thumb is that if you are still in pain three months after a wreck, ask to see a specialist, such as an orthopedist or neurosurgeon, and also visit an attorney to get his advice.

* MRI: Magnetic Resonance Imaging

LESSON 28: DON'T GIVE UP YOUR ACCIDENT CLAIM JUST BECAUSE YOU DON'T KNOW WHO HIT YOU

Drivers who cause accidents and then flee the scene (hit-and-runs) are more common than you may think. And people who drive cars with no insurance coverage (uninsureds) are not uncommon either. If you are involved in a wreck with a hit-and-run or an uninsured driver, don't just give up and assume you have to cover the resulting damages from your own pocket.

Contact your insurance company or an attorney and explain that you are making an uninsured claim, meaning someone hit you and you are not sure what, if any, insurance coverage that person has. Most states require that drivers carry **uninsured motorist coverage**, which is a type of insurance that covers you if you are the victim of an accident caused by an uninsured driver. You should have such coverage available to you in these situations.

If the driver fled the scene and you don't know who or where that person is, then you have a type of uninsurance claim known as a John Doe claim. If you were simply run off the road by a John Doe, and his car did not actually collide with your vehicle, then you must have an independent witness to the way the accident occurred in some states, such as South Carolina.

The Lesson: Don't give up on your claim in the case of a hit and run. You don't need to know all the details about making a claim against a hit-and-run or uninsured driver because your attorney will know how to make the claim. Just be aware that you still have the right to make a claim and contact your insurance company or a lawyer in these situations.

LESSON 29: ARE YOU IN BAD HANDS?

An insurance policy is a legal contract, and on your side of the contract you agree to pay the charge or premium. In return, the insurance company's side promises to reimburse you in money for certain losses you may suffer. Generally, the losses covered are property damage or personal injuries. However, almost anything of value can be the subject of an insurance contract.

Insurance policies are composed and prepared by insurance companies. They are usually long and difficult to understand. Also, these policies are worded with the object of carefully limiting what occurrences are covered by the terms of the insurance policy. The state law often dictates what types and amounts of coverage at a minimum are offered in the insurance contract. Some aspects of insurance law tend to protect the consumer's interest and others tend to protect the company's interest.

In general, insurance is a regulated area of business. The state governments have specific state agencies that deal with insurance companies and enforce the applicable regulations. However, those agencies (often called commissions) rarely get involved with individual claims. If you need help getting your insurance claim resolved you will normally need to retain an attorney.

The Lesson: Know exactly what losses your insurance policy promises to protect you or your property from suffering. Make sure to find out when your insurance company will pay benefits to you and when it will not.

LESSON 30: DON'T LET ANY UNINSURED PERSON DRIVE YOUR CAR

A client of mine, Robert, called me one day alarmed because he had been served with a lawsuit (the paperwork to begin a lawsuit is technically called a **Summons and Complaint**). His troubles began when one of his cars developed mechanical problems. Robert knew a man who lived nearby who worked on cars at a very reasonable rate, so he took the car to him for the repair.

Robert realized the mechanic had lost his driver's license for driving under the influence, so he told the mechanic not to drive the car on the highway. Of course, the mechanic later claimed he needed to test drive the vehicle and drove it on the highway anyway.

As luck would have it, the mechanic caused a collision. Robert's insurance carrier (carrier A), refused coverage because the driver was unlicensed and because he was specifically told not to drive the car.

The injured party sued the mechanic and recovered damages under her own insurance coverage. Then that insurance carrier (carrier B) sued Robert to be reimbursed for the money it had paid on the claim. This lawsuit was based on the theory that my client had negligently entrusted his car to someone he knew, or should have known, was an irresponsible and potentially impaired driver.

Fortunately, I was able to convince carrier A to provide a defense to the lawsuit in spite of its earlier denial of coverage. But Robert could have very easily found himself faced with a big bill for an attorney to defend him and an even bigger bill to reimburse insurance carrier B.

The Lesson: *Allowing someone access to your automobile can be very dangerous. It is hard to say you didn't give someone permission to drive your car when you voluntarily gave them the keys. However, if you didn't give them the keys or permission and they cause a wreck while driving your car, then your insurance company still may deny coverage and leave you to protect yourself. Your company would base this denial on the grounds that the driver was not operating the vehicle with your permission. Most liability insurance policies exclude coverage for such non-permissive drivers.*

LESSON 31: ARE YOU FULLY COVERED?

The law of most states requires that an automobile operated on the public highways have liability insurance coverage of minimum limits. For example, as of 2003, the law of South Carolina requires minimum limits of $15,000 per person and $30,000 per accident for damages due to personal injury arising out of a wreck involving that covered auto.

If your insurance agent tells you that you are "fully covered," you need to make sure you know what that means. If by "fully covered" she means only minimum limits, that is not enough to protect you adequately against claims that could arise from an auto accident you are involved in, particularly one that results in serious injuries to anyone.

Also, it is a good idea to obtain as much underinsurance coverage as you can afford. This type of coverage pays you if your personal injury damages exceed the amount of coverage available from the at-fault driver's liability policy. Because so little coverage is required, you are very likely to need underinsurance coverage if you get even moderately hurt in an automobile collision. This is very valuable coverage because it pays you, not some stranger.

Underinsurance is an optional coverage in many states, so you may have to request it. It will also require the payment of an additional premium, but it is well worth it.

The Lesson: Make sure you are adequately covered by automobile insurance and investigate what your agent means by "full coverage." Carry as much underinsurance coverage as you can afford.

LESSON 32: IF YOU BUY IT — INSURE IT

Donna was a young adult with minimal experience in business or insurance. She purchased a brand new personal watercraft (PWC) for several thousand dollars, and she financed the purchase through a bank. The bank loan officer explained to Donna that she was required to carry insurance coverage on the PWC and recommended an insurance agency.

Donna went to the insurance agency and told an employee that she needed insurance on her PWC. Donna believes she told the insurance agency representative that the PWC was financed. The agent completed the application process and an insurance company issued her a policy. Someone from the insurance company sent proof of the insurance coverage to the loan officer.

Shortly thereafter Donna was at a lake with several people she knew and a few she didn't know. She let two teenaged girls borrow her PWC, and they collided with another PWC operated by a young man. When Donna made a claim for her totaled PWC, she learned that there is more than one type of insurance. The agency had obtained liability coverage for her, but not collision coverage. Liability coverage only pays damages to someone who suffers a loss as a result of your negligence. Thus, the insurance company did not have to pay her claim for damages to the PWC.

Donna was stuck making the monthly loan payments for over two years while her lawsuit worked its way through the system. Donna was very unhappy that she had to make payments on a

PWC she couldn't use and couldn't afford to replace or have repaired.

Donna learned a hard lesson about the importance of reading legal documents like insurance applications and having a basic understanding of all types of insurance.

The Lesson: Ask your insurance agent to explain the details of your coverage. If you have a relatively new vehicle to insure, make sure you get collision coverage to protect you in the event the vehicle is damaged.

LESSON 33: INSURANCE COMMISSIONS

To understand the role insurance commissions play you need to understand that insurance is legislated and regulated at the state level. There is a movement afoot to preempt state regulation of automobile insurance by enacting federal laws that deal with all such insurance policies. However, at the time of this writing no such federal legislation had passed.

Because insurance is regulated at the state level, every state has created a regulatory body to oversee the enforcement of the insurance laws. These are usually called insurance commissions or agencies. These agencies typically oversee the way insurance companies do business, including such things as how policies are written, how premiums are charged, what risks are covered by what policies, how much capital (money) the insurance companies must set aside for the purpose of paying claims and how claims are handled.

Although insurance commissions have the authority to fine insurance companies for breaking the rules and for using unfair claims practices, this authority is exercised infrequently. As is the case in many government agencies, insurance commission employees often have close ties to the industry. Why, you may ask? The executives of the largest insurance companies, and the larger companies that own them, make millions of dollars a year in salaries and benefits. So the average government employee who works for an insurance commission makes very little income in comparison to the executives of the companies he or she is trying to regulate. If insurance commission employees hope to move from government work, with its modest compensation, into the insurance industry, with its generous compensation, they can't afford to anger their potential employers.

Additionally, as creatures of government, insurance commissions tend to be heavily influenced by politics. When you consider how much money is made, spent and invested by insurance companies, and how strong a role money plays in our politics, then their political power is obvious. The insurance industry has an army of lobbyists protecting its interests in every state capitol, as well as in Washington, DC.

Federal legislation is still a concern of the insurance industry because tax laws have a big impact on insurance companies. Tax laws affect the attractiveness of insurance products like life insurance and annuities. Also federal tax laws and other laws affect the investments of life insurance companies, the corporate structure of insurance companies, their marketing programs and taxation of executive salaries and perks.

In spite of the powerful ability of insurance companies to influence insurance commissions, those agencies can be helpful to individual consumers. Some insurance commissions have a separate department to deal with consumer complaints. Also, some states have passed laws that establish the right to appeal an insurance company decision you don't agree with to the insurance commission. Further, if an insurance commission receives enough complaints from consumers about certain actions by a particular company it will investigate the matter and sometimes issue sanctions against the company. Likewise, if an insurance commission receives complaints about a particular insurance agent or broker it may investigate and sanction that person. In severe cases the agent or broker can have his license revoked or can even be prosecuted for a crime and imprisoned.

Lesson: Contact your insurance commission any time you have a problem with an insurance company that you cannot work out with the insurance company. However, be aware that insurance commissions do not always help the consumer and you may need to hire an attorney to solve your particular problem.

LESSON 34: DON'T GIVE UP ON SOCIAL SECURITY DISABILITY

"If at first you don't succeed, try, try again". This advice may not apply to everything in life, but it definitely applies to applications for disability benefits under our federal Social Security program. If you are denied benefits in response to your first application, don't give up.

There are several reviews or appeals you can request. It has been my experience that the involvement of a competent attorney will often result in a reversal of the denial by the government agency that administers the Social Security program.

The younger you are, the harder it is to qualify for Social Security disability benefits. However, your age is only one of the factors that the agency is supposed to consider in reaching its decision. Other factors include your education, your work history, and the extent and nature of your disability.

Fortunately, most attorneys will agree to represent you on your disability claim on a contingency fee basis. Because you have to be unemployed to make a claim for social security disability, then you will obviously be unable to pay attorneys fees up front unless you have other resources. Thus, the contingency fee arrangement is most often used in these cases.

The Lesson: Experience shows that applications for Social Security benefits are often denied at the initial level, but are frequently granted after an attorney begins representing the applicant. Thus, it usually pays to keep pursuing your claim after it is denied, especially with the assistance of an attorney.

CHAPTER 6
Real Estate

INTRODUCTION: MAKE A KILLING IN REAL ESTATE, DON'T GET KILLED

Investing in real estate, like all investments, is not guaranteed to make you money. In fact, real estate is one investment that can cost you more money than you invest in it. It is a complex investment, and you need to do your homework first. However, it can be lucrative if done right.

In addition to the economic variables like interest rates that affect real estate transactions, laws have a major impact on real estate ownership and use, particularly as an investment. Laws at every level of government and regulation affect real estate investments and can often tip the balance between profit and loss. Laws on land use can likewise have a tremendous impact on real estate development or redevelopment for a new purpose.

For many of us, home ownership and perhaps property inherited within a family will be the extent of our experience in real estate. The lessons that follow represent a summary of what you will need to know to avoid land mines in these areas. For those who wish to invest in or deal in the development or conversion of use of real estate, be particularly attentive to the sections on zoning, easements and environmental considerations, and be prepared to seek out and tag many more bases in the areas of law and regulation before you score.

LESSON 35: WHAT IS A CLOSING?

A **closing** is simply a meeting of the buyer and seller of real estate at which the agreed-upon deal is concluded. Also present at this meeting will be one or more attorneys and/or paralegals*. Often the real estate agents and mortgage brokers, if any, are likewise present. Sometimes bankers or other agents of the lender will make an appearance at a closing, particularly a closing of commercial property.

During this meeting the documents necessary to complete the transfer of property and money are signed. The number of documents necessary to close a typical residential real estate sale in which a loan is involved is staggering. However, the basic, key documents are the title (also called a deed); mortgage; note; HUD settlement statement; tax forms like a W-9; title insurance binder and the certified check for payment. Many of the documents are lengthy and difficult to understand. Your basic assumption should be that the documents which are prepared or which have language dictated by the lender are worded in an effort to protect the lender's rights, not yours. Some of the documents are required by consumer-protection laws and are designed to inform you of such details as the overall cost of the loan and the interest rate being charged.

There are variations on this theme. Some closings do not involve the actual exchange of any funds and they are called **dry closings**. Some closings simply involve refinancing with no actual buyer and seller, and they are called **loan closings**. Some closings do not involve a lender and they are called **cash closings**. No matter which type of closing you are going to be sure to check with the attorney handling the closing for the exact amount of certified funds you must bring to the closing, if any. By prior arrangement or at closing, written proof that the property is covered by homeowner's insurance and has passed a termite inspection must be provided.

Arguably, the most important document in a closing is the settlement statement, called a "HUD". This two-sided form sets forth the costs being charged to the seller(s) and buyer(s). Basically, the total amount of money coming into the closing should equal the amount of money going out. However, any charges that are paid prior to the closing will be listed as "POC" or paid outside closing.

You should also insist on receiving a copy of the disbursement sheet which shows exactly what checks are being written to whom by the attorney or escrow agent. Whether you are the seller or the buyer you will want to ensure that all existing mortgages on the property are paid off and that eventually the original mortgage is marked as "paid" and returned to the seller (that process is called **satisfaction** of the mortgage). While the payment should be sent to the holder of the mortgage immediately** (to stop the accrual of interest) the actual satisfaction of the mortgage will take several weeks to be completed, but it is important to ensure that it gets done. Certainly, the original mortgage should be satisfied within six months, at the outside.

You do not necessarily have to be present at the closing at the exact same time the other party is there. Often you can come early and sign the documents and then obtain your copies later. However, in most cases it is best to try to attend the closing at the same time as the other party. A husband or wife can sign the documents for the other if a proper power of attorney is executed in advance.

The Lesson: *A closing is simply a meeting at which a real estate transaction is finalized, but you should pay close attention to the documents which you sign there to ensure that the deal that is closed is the deal that you intended to make.*

* Some states, like South Carolina, do not permit paralegals to conduct closings in the absence of an attorney. Other states allow non-lawyers to conduct real estate closings without the presence or supervision of an attorney.

** In the case of a refinance the law provides a three-day grace period in which you can change your mind and back out. Thus, the payment is not sent to the mortgage holder until after that three-day **rescission period** has run.

LESSON 36: EVER HEARD OF ZONING?

Vince, an investor, purchased a commercial building that had been foreclosed upon by a bank. He bought it at a steep discount to its appraised value. Unfortunately, he (and probably the appraiser) overlooked one crucial aspect of its value: the zoning.

The building was located right in the middle of a multi-family apartment area. The commercial activity was grandfathered* in. If the building stopped being used for commercial purposes for four months in a row, it would lose its grandfathered status. Then the building could only be used for residential use. This particular building was not nearly as valuable as a residence as it was as a business.

Whenever you consider buying a piece of real estate, be sure to confirm that the zoning regulations for the area will permit the intended use. You cannot rely on the apparent use of the property at the time you are exploring buying it because prior uses could have been grandfathered in and thus be subject to severe restrictions upon change of hands or change of use. Also, the boundary lines between one zone and another have to be drawn somewhere. Make sure you don't fall on the wrong side of the line.

Keep in mind that zoning can sometimes be changed, particularly for a large tract of land. But changes for small parcels are not generally permitted. The zoning of nearby land can adversely affect the value of your land if it is in a different zone, but near the boundary. For example, your nice retail property could drop in value if a big, ugly industrial facility were constructed within sight.

The Lesson: Be aware of zoning problems and get good advice and information before you agree to purchase any real estate.

*Exempted from the zoning restrictions because it was an existing, on-going use of the property at the time the zoning rules were implemented

LESSON 37: SOLD! BUT PUT IT IN WRITING.

Two men entered into a written contract for the purchase/sale of an old industrial building for $600,000. They literally wrote the contract on a napkin. When the appraiser was performing the appraisal, which was required by the commercial lender, he found partially buried barrels of what appeared to be hazardous waste.

Needless to say, a dispute erupted over whose responsibility it was to clean up the waste and whether the purchase had to proceed by the date indicated on the napkin or whether the buyer had the right to delay while the wastes were being evaluated.

As a result, both sides hired lawyers and filed lawsuits. They accumulated big litigation bills and neither side was happy with the outcome.

This case is especially amazing because form real estate purchase contracts are easily obtained and specifically cover contingencies like those encountered by these businessmen.

The Lesson: Avoid a costly lawsuit by completing a comprehensively written contract for the purchase or sale of real estate. Have a real estate expert or attorney review all real estate purchase contracts.

LESSON 38: DON'T LEAVE REAL ESTATE *IN FEE* TO SOMEONE WHO NEEDS IT *IN TRUST*.

I represented a senior citizen, Linda, who was involved in a serious car accident in which she sustained a bad injury, putting her into a wheelchair for the rest of her life. Fortunately, there was a good deal of insurance coverage available, and Linda obtained a substantial recovery.

Linda was resourceful enough to realize that this was a once-in-a-lifetime opportunity, and she saved and invested the proceeds instead of spending them like so many do. She hoped to use a portion of the funds to help her two sons, who needed it. One in particular was illiterate, unsophisticated and barely able to earn a living.

Linda decided to buy a small house and give it to her disadvantaged son so he would always have a home. That was a good idea, but she made the mistake of giving the son complete and total ownership (often called **in fee**). After Linda died, the son became involved with some bad people who took advantage of his naiveté. They talked him into taking out a loan secured with a mortgage on the house. And then the son became completely disabled and couldn't make his mortgage payments.

If Linda had given the house to her son *in trust*, instead of *in fee*, he wouldn't have been able to put a mortgage on it, and he would still have a place to live.

The Lesson: When providing for loved ones by giving them real estate, be careful. If they are unable to take care of themselves, someone else should be given the power to control the real estate. If you do not want the loved one to sell the real estate, then you need to take certain legal precautions, such as putting the title in trust.

LESSON 39: KILLER TERMITES?

When can termites be killers? When they kill a real estate deal. Every house is sold with a contract that requires a **clear termite letter**. A termite letter is simply a written report from a pest control expert that says the expert found no live termites in the structure and sets forth any termite damage discovered. The seller usually has to repair the damage before the closing of the sale.

A client of mine, Ned, bought a house for the purpose of improving it and reselling it at a profit. He had a termite inspection done before he purchased it. When he resold it, the buyer had another termite inspection done by a different inspector. Neither termite inspector found live termites, but both found old termite damage. The buyers also had a home inspection done by a professional home inspector, who didn't find any live termites either. However, when the new owners began renovations, they discovered live termites.

Ned, who had relied on the professionals, ended up getting sued for fraud and failure to disclose. Needless to say, he didn't make a profit on that deal. One rule of thumb you can follow is that termites follow water. If a house has a water drainage problem, it will usually have termites.

The Lesson: *When it comes to real estate, termites can be killers.*

LESSON 40: THIS STINKS! POLLUTION PROBLEMS WITH REAL ESTATE

Failure to disclose nearby environmental blights in a real estate transaction is a growing source of legal disputes. One case in which I was involved had a very interesting situation.

A disabled man, Jim, was shown a house in a modest subdivision that was very reasonably priced and could easily be modified to meet his physical requirements. Jim was from out-of-town and was not familiar with the area surrounding this subdivision. A few months after he closed the purchase of the house, Jim overheard some people talking about a nearby landfill. He was surprised to learn there was one in the area because none of the people involved in the real estate transaction had mentioned it.

However, Jim's surprise turned to distress when the garbage dump grew so high that he could see it from his house, particularly when the vegetation died back in the winter. Unfortunately, he couldn't afford to hire attorneys to fight the lengthy and uncertain battle to recover damages for the failure to disclose.

In a similar case, a client of mine bought a house and large lot without knowing that a prior owner had used underground storage tanks for gasoline or some other petroleum product. Under applicable laws and regulations, certain testing and reporting is required when those tanks are abandoned.

My client had to pay for the required testing and reporting. He is negotiating with the prior owner in hopes of being reimbursed, but the outcome is not clear.

Again, don't let some problem that is out of sight and out of mind cause you to pay out of your pocket. Find it before you close the purchase of the real estate when you can deal with it more easily.

The Lesson: *The law is not clear on how close an environmental problem has to be to a parcel of real estate before the seller is obligated to disclose its existence to a potential buyer. Given the lack of clear guidance, a seller should generally disclose more than he would wish. Likewise, a buyer should assume that less than he wants is being disclosed. In short, in any real estate transaction, keep your eyes wide open.*

LESSON 41: WHAT IS AN EASEMENT?

Sarah and Bob bought a house located in a subdivision which was developed three decades earlier. Their lot was one of the last two created and built upon. The sewer line from their house was out of sight and thus out of mind. They didn't ask about it and the seller didn't volunteer any information about it.

Unfortunately, the sewer line presented three major problems. First, it was unsound and began to collapse causing backups. Second, it was not legally connected to the public sewer agency's system and wasn't in compliance with its specifications. And third, it passed underground beneath their neighbor's concrete driveway.

A major issue arose when Sara and Bob wanted to replace the old sewer pipe and the neighbor did not want his driveway torn up. The neighbor's deed made no specific mention of the sewer line or any **easement** for it.

What is an easement? An easement is a liberty, privilege or advantage which one may hold in the lands of another. The holder of an easement has the right to use a tract of land for a special purpose, but has no right to possess and enjoy the tract of land.

Although most easements are created by written language in a deed, they may also be created by the way the land was subdivided and/or used. The courts create easements to prevent lots from being landlocked. The law assumes that all landowners should have some means of access to their land. If a particular roadway has been used continuously for 20 years or more, the courts will hold that an easement was created by use. Thus, even though the adjoining landowners who used the road never paid any money to the owner of the tract over which the roadway ran for the easement, the courts will declare that such an easement exists nonetheless.

Although Sarah and Bob did not have a piece of paper that specifically granted them the right to maintain a sewer line across their neighbor's land, a judge would likely hold that they did in fact have that right because of the circumstances. However, they would still have to replace the pipe and meet the requirements of the public sewer agency for connecting to the public sewer system, and any disturbance of the neighbor's property would have to be set right at their expense.

One way of viewing easements is that the law of easements is really just the application of common sense. We all live in interdependence with our neighbors (except perhaps in the Alaska bush) and there has to be some cooperation of adjoining landowners, even if it imposes somewhat on the exclusive use and possession of their land. Without easements our modern civilization, with its dependence on utility systems, transportation systems and free commerce, would grind to a stagnant halt.

The Lesson: Adjoining landowners may have limited rights to cross each other's property with a driveway or utility, even if no legal paper specifically grants that right. Whenever you purchase real estate explore the status of such easements and rights-of-way.

LESSON 42: MECHANIC'S LIEN

Once a carpenter, plumber, electrician or other tradesman has completed his work on your construction project (typically a new house), he can file a lien against your title to ensure payment of the bill. There are strict time limits on how soon after a workman (in legal language, **mechanic**) completes the job a lien must be filed and then enforced with a lawsuit.

If you are a subcontractor on a construction project, you should always file a mechanic's lien as soon as you suspect that you may not be fully or promply paid. And if you are an owner, you have to be aware that the lien will attach to your title even if it is the primary contractor (general contractor) who is supposed to pay the subcontractor.

The Lesson: Protect your rights by seeking legal counsel to review the construction contracts before you sign them and as soon as your construction project hits rough waters. Your rights will be affected by the written contracts and the laws concerning mechanics' liens. Additionally, if you are financing the project, there will be more legal issues dealing with the lender and its contracts.

CHAPTER 7
Death and Taxes

INTRODUCTION: HOW TO BE SURE YOU ARE READY, LEGALLY

"Our new Constitution is now established and has an appearance that promises permanency; but in this world nothing can be said to be certain but death and taxes."

—Benjamin Franklin (1706-1790)

The death of a loved one or business partner can create legal chaos for you. The emotional toll is usually increased by the legal mess known as **probate**, and coping with all those burdens can overwhelm even the strongest person.

Although death may be a certainty, the exact date and time is an unknown. Because of this few of us get around to preparing a last will and testament. We simply do not want to confront our own mortality.

It may be trite, but it's true, that you can't take it with you when you die. The good news is that when you depart for greener pastures your financial problems stay behind; the bad news is that your family may be stuck with those problems. Issues that often arise after someone dies are: who pays the debts, who gets the personal and real property, who resolves disputes among family members or other heirs, who interprets the last will and testament, what do you do with heavily mortgaged property, and who pays the funeral bill? These are some of the issues that are resolved through a process called probate. Dealing with these matters is so unique and important that a separate court was created to oversee these difficult decisions, typically called **The Probate Court**. However, other courts can decide some issues that arise in an estate and the decisions of the probate court can be appealed to higher courts.

After the religious rites and family gatherings are over it is time for someone to find the deceased's **Last Will and Testament** (or determine that one doesn't exist) and secure the property from theft or other adverse consequences. The Will nominates someone to act as the **Personal Representative** (previously called the **Executor**). This person takes charge of the property, including any documents that may be important. The Probate Court will require you to complete one or more forms that call for you to list all property of significant value, financial accounts, life insurance policies and debts. Other documents will have to be completed and approved by the court. Also, disputes over who gets what may have to be resolved by the court.

If you are a beneficiary or heir of a Will and do not like the results that should come from its language, then you should go consult with an attorney at once. There are a variety of measures that you can take to modify the outcome of provisions in a Will. However, it is not necessary to challenge the validity of the entire Will just because you do not like one part of it. For example, you can refuse to accept an item that the Will gives to you. Why would you do this? If the item was a tract of contaminated land or if the item produced undesirable tax consequences, you might want to refuse it.

Most estates involve modest amounts of property and a significant amount of paperwork. The personal representative gets very modest compensation for his or her efforts. Yet occasionally an estate involves enough property to create disputes among potential heirs or creditors. Needless to say the land of probate can be strewn with headaches and hassles.

LESSON 43: LEARN WHAT A LAST WILL AND TESTAMENT PROVIDES

A **Last Will and Testament**, or simply "Will," is a written expression of your desires for how your property will be distributed once you have died. The law requires that a Will be signed in the presence of witnesses, and the interpretation of certain words and phrases used in Wills has been established in the case law over the decades. Thus, the proper preparation and signing of a Will is carefully set forth by the law; the more complicated the Will, the more complicated the legal rules that apply.

A Will can also indicate your preference for custodian, guardian or trustee for your minor children and/or for their possesions and inheritance in the case of your death. However, a court will make an independent ruling on who to appoint as custodian. The judge will make this decision based on his or her perception of what is in the best interests of your children. But knowing your preference will be important to the judge making the custodial decision.

If you don't have a Will when you die, your property could go to an estranged spouse, an undeserving child, or a disliked relative. Also, failing to have a proper Will can cause much of your estate's assets to be paid to creditors or the state and federal governments. You probably wouldn't deliberately name Uncle Sam as your heir, so don't unconsciously allow that to happen by not making a proper Will.

A Will is not a power of attorney (refer to Lesson 10 for an explanation). Any part of a Will or the entire document can be changed by you prior to your death. So don't make the mistake of thinking that a Personal Representative named in a Will has any legal rights or responsibilities before the maker of the Will dies.

If you read John Grisham's book, The Testament, you will get a vivid illustration of the rule that anyone can change his Will at anytime prior to death

The Lesson: *Write a Will so your wishes will be followed after your death. If you don't, you may be rewarding people other than your lovedones. Tell your Personal Representative that you have named him, but don't burden him with extra instructions that could tie his hands or compromise your Will in court. Instead, have a lawyer prepare your will and incorporate all of your important wishes into it.*

LESSON 44: ARE YOU AN EXECUTOR OF AN ESTATE?

When someone dies, a spouse or relative usually takes legal responsibility for the property (called an **estate**) owned by the deceased. A part of those responsibilities is the debts of the deceased. The Probate Court will formally appoint someone to handle these things and that person in most states is called a Personal Representative (PR), often formerly called the Executor or Executrix. When you are appointed as a PR, the Probate Court gives you guidance on what to do. However, be careful not to pay any bills or debts of the deceased until you are certain it is necessary. Of course, the providers of various services, such as utilities, cable TV or newspaper delivery to the deceased should be notified of the death so those services can be discontinued.

The way debts of a deceased are generally handled in most states is that the debtor should make a formal, written claim for the debt that is sent either to the Probate Court or the PR. The PR should then wait until the creditor period has run so he can determine whether there are sufficient funds in the estate to pay all the bills. If there are sufficient funds and the PR feels the debts are valid, then the claims are formally "allowed" or accepted by the PR and paid. If not, the PR "disallows" the debtor's claim, either wholly or partially. If the creditor wishes to contest the disallowance, he must request a hearing in the Probate Court. At the hearing, the Probate Judge decides what portion, if any, of the debts the estate will pay.

When someone dies, resist the urge to pay the bills of the deceased immediately, unless they are for ongoing expenses that must be met, like mortgage payments. For those payments that you think should be made, call the creditor and try to get the payments deferred until after you get the estate formally opened at the Probate Court. Then follow the guidance of the Court or an attorney.

The Lesson: Understand that you are under no legal obligations to pay the debts of the deceased from your own funds. Even if you have been appointed the PR, you should not pay any debts of the deceased with your personal funds unless that is the only way to retain an asset that you stand to inherit. It is always possible that you will not be reimbursed for any such personal payments of estate debts. Get the Probate Court or an attorney to guide you on the handling of the estate.

LESSON 45: "RENDER THEREFORE UNTO CAESAR THE THINGS WHICH ARE CAESAR'S..."

— MATTHEW 22:21

Everyone hates paying taxes. I imagine that even IRS agents grumble about it from time to time. In spite of all the promises of politicians, our tax laws remain very complicated and thus a legal burden to the average citizen. When you need help, whom do you call?

The two primary professionals we usually call for tax help are accountants and tax attorneys. What's the difference? The biggest difference, in my mind, is that no attorney-client privilege guards what you tell your accountant, but it does guard what you tell your attorney. This privilege protects you from having your tax attorney testify against you. I also believe that most accountants have a very different approach to solving tax problems than do most attorneys.

It seems that accountants are usually more pragmatic than tax attorneys, but they may not understand all the nuances of the tax laws and regulations. Accountants and tax attorneys often approach tax questions from different perspectives, although they usually arrive at the same answers. Generally, accountants charge lower hourly rates than tax attorneys. Because tax problems are complex and can be costly, you need to weigh carefully whether to use a less expensive accountant or a more expensive tax attorney, or both.

The so-called death tax has received lots of media attention lately. Recently, the Congress passed and the President signed dramatic changes to the laws governing death taxes (more appropriately called "estate taxes"). The changes are supposedly going to phase out all estate taxes over the years until 2010, when they are currently scheduled to cease. Other changes to the tax laws will probably negate much of these tax savings.

If your total net assets could exceed a million dollars upon your death, then you need to see an estate tax professional. Proper estate planning can help your heirs from being hit with taxes upon the assets they inherit from you. Also, estate planning can help you support charitable organizations with the money that would otherwise go to pay estate taxes.

The Lesson: If you are an heir of an estate that is worth $1,000,000 or more, you should seek tax advice immediately. Certain legal steps can be taken early in the probate process to help you minimize the tax burden.

LESSON 46: "NO ASSETS" MEANS NO HASSLES

Have you ever heard the saying, "He died with nothing but the clothes on his back." Someone like that does not leave any assets behind for anyone to worry about. But when someone dies with significant assets, there are often legal problems with disposing of those assets. Such problems can be avoided.

The heirs of a deceased will avoid most of the legal land mines hidden in the legal process known as probate if the deceased titled assets jointly (with right of survivorship) or actually gave away property before passing away. If all the significant assets in an estate are titled jointly, then the probate court can treat the estate as a **no-asset estate** that allows a streamlined process to be used in closing out the estate file.

A person desiring to avoid probate can also give away all of her assets, outright or in trust, prior to her death. This is not, however, as simple as it seems. If you have assets involving real estate or more than $100,000 in financial accounts, then you should seek the advice of a competent tax professional before you transfer any assets. Also, be aware that both federal and state governments have restrictions on providing Medicaid to people who have given away assets.

Giving away assets by way of a Living Trust can lead you into dangerous legal territory. Do not try to prepare any type of trust on your own, and be skeptical of Living Trust seminars, books, and tapes. Transferring assets in trust without competent legal advice is like walking through a minefield with a blindfold on.

The Lesson: *No-asset estates are easy to probate, but creating one by transferring assets is tricky. Get legal advice so that you, in fact, create a no-asset estate instead of a legal minefield.*

LESSON 47: THY WILL BE DONE

People are often confused about what a **Will** is and what it can do. A person's Last Will and Testament is of little use until he or she dies. While the maker of the Will is alive, the Will has no effect on their property or children. Likewise, heirs and beneficiaries named in a Will have absolutely no rights to the property prior to the death of the maker of the Will. Don't mistake the qualities of Wills for those of Deeds, which are documents that pass ownership of real estate from one living person to another living person. Likewise, don't confuse a Will and a Power of Attorney, which is a document that gives one living person the power and authority to handle another living person's affairs. A Will simply expresses how you want your property disposed of after your death.

A Will cannot give custody of a child or an incompetent adult to another person. You can express guidance for a court on that issue in your Will, but the judge is still obligated to make a custody decision that is in the best interest of the child or incompetent adult.

A Will basically sets forth your desires for the disposal of your property once you die. While a Will cannot control the disposition of assets forever, it can severely restrict that disposition for many years. Courts don't generally want a deceased person's wishes to control people or their use of property for too long a period and, thus, tend to interpret Wills so that the control of property is finite. But exactly how long you can control the course of property use and ownership into the future is impossible to say.

If you are determined to extend your control over property for long after you have died, then you will need the help of a sharp attorney who is a specialist in trusts and estates.

Attorneys discourage people from attempting to control the disposition of real estate for long periods after their deaths because such legal arrangements, whether made in a Will or Trust, can lead to unexpected negative tax consequences. Also, such arrangements can make it impossible for real estate to be sold or developed, resulting in it sitting idle for many years. Almost every town in South Carolina has one or more houses that were tied up by the language in a Will and are abandoned eyesores. Heirs often don't have the funds or inclination to maintain old houses while they wait for their ancestor's restrictions to expire. Consequently, the houses sit and decay.

The Lesson: To make sure you accomplish your goals for your assets, including property, you need to understand clearly what a Will can and cannot do. If you have substantial assets, you also need to consult a competent attorney who specializes in trusts, estates and taxes.

CHAPTER 8

Divorce

INTRODUCTION: HOW TO KEEP THE GOLDMINE AND AVOID THE SHAFT

The legal, financial, emotional and logistical worries of a divorce take a heavy toll on everyone involved. There are resources available to help you deal with the emotional challenges of divorce, and I urge you to seek them out. However, this chapter is an attempt to help you dodge some of the land mines that the legal aspects of divorce will threaten you with.

Divorce was once strongly discouraged in the western world. The Church of England was created because King Henry the Eighth wanted a divorce, but the Roman Catholic Church would not grant him one. When the Pope refused to agree to the King's request, he created his own state church and had his handpicked Bishop grant him a divorce. During the twentieth century divorce became more and more common in the English-speaking world, with a large increase in the 1970s. In order to obtain a divorce prior to that time you typically had to have grounds such as adultery, abandonment or physical cruelty.

During the 1960s, 1970s and 1980s, more and more states created no-fault grounds for divorce. In the more liberal states you only had to claim incompatibility, but in more conservative states you had to prove a certain period of separation. For example, in South

Carolina you have to prove actual, continuous physical separation, without cohabitation, for at least one year.

Some states that recognize physical cruelty as grounds for a divorce do not recognize mental cruelty. This is unfortunate in my opinion. Nonetheless, more and more victims of abusive relationships, whether the abuse is physical, emotional, verbal, sexual, financial or a combination, are divorcing the abusive spouse to save their sanity and sometimes their lives. For more information about abuse see related references listed in Appendix G.

Divorce cases are complicated because people are complicated. We all live complex lives, and it is difficult to part two or more lives that have been intertwined by marriage and familial relationships.

If divorce seems likely in your future, keep your eyes and ears open and pick a good divorce lawyer or you could become the victim of a nasty battle.

LESSON 48: THE FAMILY COURT SYSTEM

Divorce, custody, child support and similar cases are handled in many states in a special court, often called a **Family Court**. In other states the regular trial courts handle those cases. However, in most jurisdictions family law cases are decided by judges, not juries. Nonetheless, a few states allow juries to decide some aspects of these cases.

Family Courts may also decide cases such as juvenile crime cases and name changes. Family law litigation has become much more common over the last several decades. This rapid increase in divorce, custody, child support and juvenile criminal cases is often described as an explosion. Thus, there is a definite need for specialized courts to deal with these cases. There are those who argue that Family Court judges become too jaded to make good decisions and that the right to a jury trial should always be available to litigants in these cases, but a major change in this court system seems unlikely to occur soon.

In addition to having different systems of courts, states also have different laws concerning family law issues. For example, it is very easy to get a no-fault divorce in Georgia, Nevada, and Washington State. However, in South Carolina, to the contrary, you have to attend a hearing and present at least one witness before you can be awarded a no-fault divorce. Also, some states require that you live in the state for a year before you have access to its courts for a divorce, while others only require a few weeks or months.

Laws concerning alimony, child support, and marital property distribution also vary tremendously from state to state. The biggest difference is that some states are community property states and some are not. In community property states each spouse automatically has a one-half interest in all marital property (property acquired during the marriage). In other states the spouse's interest in marital property is determined by the court based on such factors as: his or her contribution to the acquisition of the property; his or her contribution to the marriage; fault or absence of fault; length of the marriage; special needs of a spouse and the spouse's ability to support oneself. The general tendency of the courts is to split the property 50/50 if the couple has been married for 10 or more years. Inheritances and gifts are usually not marital property, but there are exceptions to that rule (as with most legal rules).

Child-support law varies from state to state, with some states requiring that a greater percentage of a spouse's income go to child support than others. In some states the courts must apply a formula based on the parties' respective income levels that is specific and consistent. Others allow the courts more discretion in setting child support levels. While there is a federal law that establishes a national child support collection system, the basic support amounts are set according to the state with jurisdiction over the child to be supported. Interstate collection of child support is typically slow, cumbersome and inconsistent.

Litigation in family court is often very stressful, complex, time-intensive and consequently expensive. Often feelings of betrayal, revenge, guilt and failure color the cases. Divorce always causes a net loss economically because two homes are more expensive to maintain than one. It is not unusual for a middle or working class family to be bankrupt after a divorce. Divorce contributes to the poverty and homelessness of many people, including children. But, for the foreseeable future, divorce is here to stay. If you find yourself facing a divorce or other Family Court case I strongly recommend that you learn as much as possible about the particular laws that apply to your case. Details are very important in family law cases, as is financial information. Try to gather as much evidence as you can before you walk into a family courtroom because it truly is a legal minefield.

The Lesson: The Family Court system, particularly as it applies to divorce and child custody, is complex and generally produces results that are, to varying degrees, unsatisfactory to every party involved. For this reason you should work hard to negotiate an amicable, legally valid settlement which can be presented to the court for approval. However, prior to agreeing to any terms in a settlement, document your case as thoroughly as you can, choose your attorney carefully and keep a lid on your expectations. While it is always desirable to settle a Family Court case, you must do the preparation to insure the terms are fair and reasonable to you. If you have to go to trial, be prepared for disappointing results.

LESSON 49: DON'T FORGET THE HOUSE PAYMENT

Barbara separated from her husband when he left the marital home. She later discovered that several months before he left, he stopped making the mortgage payments. And after he left, he managed to keep the foreclosure notices from being received by her. Then the house burned to the ground.

The fire insurance company that carried the fire insurance on the home began an investigation of her claim. It discovered that the home had been foreclosed upon and the court had issued an order that transferred the title of the home to the mortgage company.

Because my client was no longer the legal title-holder to the real estate, she could not pursue the fire insurance claim. As her attorney, I tried to get the court to reopen the foreclosure case, but it refused. Her divorce was already final at that point, so she was at a dead end.

The Lesson: Always keep track of the status of your mortgage and other important payments, especially if you separate from your spouse.

LESSON 50: CUSTODY CHANGES CAN BE DANGEROUS

Custody issues concerning minor children can be extremely tough to handle. Because parents and grandparents usually have strong feelings of love and responsibility for their children or grandchildren, custody battles are always highly emotional. And those feelings of love and responsibility often foster feelings of hate towards anyone trying to take custody away and guilt over any alleged or perceived failings in the proper care of the children.

I've had clients who voluntarily relinquished custody of their children to the other parent or to the grandparents due to financial hardship, only to find that the temporary custodians refused to return the children later when my clients were in a better financial position.

I've even had a mother almost be denied custody of her children when they were in the hands of an aunt and uncle. The father had legal custody and had turned over *de facto* or actual custody to the aunt and uncle while he was stationed overseas with the military. The father was killed in a car wreck while serving overseas. When the mother asked for the return of the children, the aunt and uncle refused. Litigation ensued, but it took several months and thousands of dollars for the mother to regain custody of her children.

I also know of a father who accepted the physical custody of his children when the mother no longer wanted custody of them. He stopped paying child support but took no court action to change the legal custody. Later, the mother demanded them back and asked the Family Court to hold him in contempt for not paying child support. He was in a very perilous position and could have gone to jail if he had been found in contempt.

The Lesson: Don't ever violate a formal custody order issued by a court without immediately retaining an attorney to transfer the custody legally. Likewise, be warned that temporary custody changes can become permanent custody changes.

LESSON 51: IN DIVORCE, KNOWLEDGE IS POWER!

It is amazing how many wives in this day and age do not know how much money their husbands make. Whether her husband is a construction worker or a business executive, many a wife just doesn't know the amount of his actual income, and may not have any idea what he spends his pay on, whether it is stocks, gambling, booze, other women, cars, bass boats, real estate or clothes. Occasionally, it is the wives who make and spend the money and the husbands who don't have a clue.

Because a major part of any divorce is dividing the marital property and liabilities, it is important to know your spouse's true financial situation. Many spouses involved in divorces have tried to hide at least some of their income and/or assets. Once you have separated from your spouse it can be very difficult to determine the truth on these issues.

Thus, you should always get your own copy of the tax returns each year, and you should study the return to try to get a clear picture of your joint financial situation. Then if you separate from your spouse, you will easily be able to explain your finances to your attorney who, in turn, can ensure you receive all you are entitled to in the divorce.

Sometimes tax returns will either not be filed or will be inaccurate. If your spouse gets paid in cash, for example as a subcontractor on a construction job, it can be very hard to prove in court what he or she makes in actual dollars. Your best bet is probably to keep track of who is paying your spouse so you can subpoena the employer to testify in Family Court. Also, if your spouse makes any loan applications keep a copy of the application for your records because it will document his or her income.

The Lesson: *When it comes to your marital finances, what you don't know can hurt you. Without this knowledge, you will not get your fair share of marital assets in a divorce.*

LESSON 52: PROTECT YOUR MONEY

Many people who divorce see it coming, but given the emotional turmoil they are in, it is not surprising that they fail to take sufficient steps to protect their finances from the machinations of their estranged spouses.

One of the precautions that spouses typically fail to take is closing or depleting joint accounts of all types. Credit card accounts can be difficult because any existing balance will prevent them from being closed. But you should be able to get the account coded so that no further charges can be made. If you don't feel comfortable about completely depleting a joint account, then at least do so by one-half the balance.

A joint account that is often overlooked is a checking account credit line, usually established to prevent bounced checks. Unfortunately, the first spouse to think of it can use the entire line of credit by withdrawing cash, yet the other spouse is still liable on the debt to the bank.

The Lesson: *As soon as you hit the choppy seas of marital discord, you should close, suspend or deplete your joint accounts.*

LESSON 53: POSSESSION IS 9/10THS OF THE LAW

It really doesn't sound fair, but often the party who has possession of anything over which a legal dispute has arisen has an advantage in the struggle. For example, in a child custody dispute, the person who has the physical custody of the child at the outset of the dispute usually has a distinct advantage. Of course, the courts will not reward kidnapping, but if your physical custody of the child is not illegal, you will be better off in the custody battle that ensues.

Another example is that possession of real estate or other property gives you several advantages in a legal dispute over that property. It is easy for you to protect the asset from harm from a third party, and it is easy for you to have the property appraised. In addition, it is often an advantage to be able to use and enjoy the property during the pending dispute.

A final example of the power of possession is a case in which a Family Court judge awarded a spouse involved in a divorce the temporary custody and control of a dog and horse. In this case, she sold the horse and had the dog put to sleep. While the husband was convinced she took those actions just for spite, it was difficult to prove because she had plausible reasons for why she had to take them.

The Lesson: *Try to maintain possession over any property that is the subject of a legal dispute. Having physical possession gives you the ability to preserve, appraise, use and protect the property during the pendency of the lawsuit.*

CHAPTER **9**

The Business of Business

INTRODUCTION: YOU WANT TO MAKE MONEY, NOT LOSE IT!

We go into business to make money, not lose it. And while we are often aware of the need to have a lawyer set up the legal framework of our business or corporation, after that initial meeting we often avoid lawyers like they are computer viruses. But experienced and successful business people know that a good lawyer is an invaluable partner in their business ventures. In fact, many CEOs of large, successful companies began working as in-house counsel for their companies.

You have to assume that your business partners, clients, customers and competitors know more about the law than you do. They are either being advised by lawyers or have been in the past, and you should be just as prepared. Without an understanding of the legal ramifications of every business contract or deal you enter into, you are walking blindfolded through a minefield. Avoid becoming a casualty by staying informed and obtaining legal representation whenever necessary.

An experienced lawyer once told me that he has seen the same lifecycle of a business deal repeated over and over. At the birth of a business, one partner usually contributes the money and the other partner offers his experience. In most cases, at the demise of the business, the one with the experience walks away with money, and the one who had the money ends up with a painful experience. Legal representation can help you avoid being the one who gets the painful experience.

A good written contract is just one of the many legal documents that can help you in business. Just as good fences make good neighbors, good contracts make good business deals. While a written contract cannot prevent a business from falling apart, it can prevent the failure from harming you more than one of your partners. A written contract can also save you money on litigation costs by preventing misunderstandings that have to be resolved in court. Mean what you say and say what you mean, in writing.

LESSON 54: BEWARE OF BAD BUSINESS PARTNERS

Steve's case

Steve, who was well educated and very bright, went into business with a couple of people who claimed to have the know-how to manufacture and sell small trailers, called tow dollies. Because they didn't have the capital to expand the business past the very early stages, they talked Steve into providing the capital in the form of cash and bank loans that he personally guaranteed.

A personal guarantee is a written contract that binds the guarantor to pay bills created by another party, usually a business the guarantor owns. Banks and suppliers typically require partners or corporate owners to sign guarantees for loans or credit to their businesses.

Unfortunately, Steve relied completely on what he was told by these persuasive entrepreneurs. He didn't receive any independent advice on limiting his risk or protecting his interest in the venture. He was an easy victim of mismanagement or fraud by his partners.

After a year, and a few tow dollies later, the business collapsed and left Steve holding the bag to the tune of a half million dollars in bank debt. Steve didn't have any of the financial records of the company, and the entrepreneurs claimed the records were lost. He had stepped onto a legal land mine.

When Steve finally did consult a lawyer, all the assets of the company were gone, and the one company document he had received from his partners did not even create the legal entity Steve thought it had .

Steve was left with the difficult decision of whether to bring an expensive lawsuit against his former partners, who had few ready assets, and one of whom had filed for bankruptcy. Because there were no documents, the trial would have boiled down to a swearing contest. And, if he did win the swearing contest in court, all he would likely get would be a judgment for money. Judgments can be very hard to collect, especially if the person owns no equity in real estate to pursue.

The Lesson: In a business deal, relying on what someone else tells you can be an expensive mistake. Insist on written documentation of every aspect of the business. Carefully monitor how the money you invest is being spent.

LESSON 55: BEWARE OF BAD CUSTOMERS

Rick's Case

Rick, a hard-working client of mine, ran his own small business doing grading, hauling, back-hoe projects and related work. He bid upon and was awarded a job demolishing some old industrial buildings and hauling them off.

One of the people who hired Rick told him he could simply haul the refuse down the road a short distance to a vacant piece of property. Of course, Rick thought that having a close disposal place would save him considerable time and money. Unfortunately, the owner of the vacant property had never granted permission to Rick or his customer for the disposal of such debris upon his land. Law enforcement and environmental officials were called, and Rick faced criminal prosecution for unlawful dumping. He also faced administrative penalties for improper disposal of asbestos, which was found in the dumped materials.

Unbeknownst to my client, the old building he was demolishing contained friable asbestos, a carcinogenic substance. He was ordered to remove the hazardous material immediately from the site and to pay for its proper disposal. Consequently, Rick incurred great expense for the extra time, equipment, and disposal fees the clean-up required.

What had seemed like a legitimate, profitable project to Rick quickly became a huge financial burden. With legal assistance, Rick was able to get the administrative penalty lowered, but his only defense was ignorance. And, as the saying goes, ignorance of the law is no excuse.

Rick believed that the people who hired him knew the building contained asbestos, but intentionally failed to disclose it. However, he did not have any proof. As a result, he was never reimbursed for all his added expenses.

Encountering hazardous waste on a job site is one of the risks that should always be covered in a business contract. And, of course, you should insist on full disclosure of hazardous materials whenever you work at a job site, especially one with which you are not completely familiar. Finally, never assume you can dump waste materials on anyone's property without written permission from the owner.

The Lesson: *A reasonable dose of prevention, such as avoiding bad business customers, can avoid a very expensive cure!*

LESSON 56: LEAVING IS NOT ALWAYS EASY

Fred went into business with a partner to sell mobile homes. To operate, they had to establish accounts with various suppliers. The suppliers wisely required Fred and his partner to sign personal guarantees of the accounts.

When Fred decided to exit the business, he overlooked an important detail — he didn't cancel the guarantees to the suppliers. Fred's partner kept the business going for eight more months and ran up substantial charges for supplies on the accounts. When the business failed and the partner vamoosed, the suppliers sued Fred.

If a guarantee has a cancellation clause, it must be followed precisely; however, you may still be responsible for the balance due at the time you cancelled the guarantee. The same rule applies to other authorizations and joint obligations you may have signed. When exiting a business, remember to formally notify all banks, credit card companies and other creditors that you are no longer responsible for the business debts.

The Lesson: Be careful whom you go into business with because leaving them may not be easy. Make sure to cancel any personal guarantees before you exit the business. If you are involved in a very complex business or one involving high potential liability, contact an attorney to obtain guidance on other steps you can take to limit your liability.

LESSON 57: MAKE CONTACTS, BUT ALSO MAKE CONTRACTS

A common cause of legal problems in business deals is the failure of the parties to write down their agreement or, in other words, make a written contract. It is human nature to believe that you and your business partner(s) fully understand each other, especially when you are at the beginning of a business relationship. You believe you can trust the other person to live up to his word. You are happy that you are in agreement with the other person and that you are embarking on a mutually advantageous venture.

However, the circumstances of people's lives and their businesses change. Interest rates, growth rates, technology, and prices of materials are just a sampling of business variables that tend to change over time. A change in a partner's life will affect you, too.

The memories and interests of owners are also inclined to diverge as a business progresses. You might walk into the office one day and discover that you no longer see eye to eye with your associates. Then small disagreements grow into large disagreements and you find yourself in a lawyer's office. For example, you and your partner may disagree over which of the out-of-pocket expenses you each have incurred for gas, hotel bills, supplies, etc., should be reimbursed from business assets. Without a written contract, disagreements are likely to arise.

The Lesson: Without a written contract to refer to, your case in court would simply amount to a swearing contest. Then you will kick yourself for not putting your agreement in writing.

LESSON 58: TALK IS CHEAP — TRY TO GET PROMISES IN WRITING

John, an older man, orally negotiated the terms of his employment contract with his new employer. He gave his employer's representative a copy of a written contract that he wanted the employer to agree to. During his negotiations, the representative assured John he would submit the proposed contract to his superior and they would provide him with a written contract with the same or similar terms. Of course, John never received the promised written contract, and he started working with the belief that his new employer had agreed to his contract terms.

What made having a written contract so very important to John was the nature of his business. He worked as a food broker and represented particular lines of food or brands. The producers of those lines tended to be loyal to their brokers, so the new employer knew he would gain those particular food companies as clients if he hired John.

The new employer later fired John and tried to give his lines to a new, younger broker. But his plan didn't work because John's lines (companies) refused to work with the new broker, so John was rehired a few days later.

The employer began making life difficult for John, whose health had been declining. Eventually, the employer pressured John to retire, but he also held onto John's lines. John received nothing in return for those lines upon his retirement.

John was certain he was discriminated against because of his age, and that he was tricked into giving up his lines. Likewise, John was not compensated as fully as he had delineated in his contract proposal. Without a written contract, there wasn't much John could do about his forced retirement. He couldn't believe that at the end of his long career he had been so badly mistreated. But, if he had simply insisted on a written contract before he began working, he could have avoided this legal land mine.

The Lesson: *Oral business contracts, especialy oral employment contracts, are difficult to enforce. Always get important contract terms in writing.*

LESSON 59: A GOOD DEAL? GET IT IN WRITING

Dave, who was an immigrant with limited formal education, bought a taco stand from a woman who made oral representations that the business was very profitable. She used an attorney to draw up a purchase contract that detailed the series of payments Dave would have to make, but failed to include any representations about either the profitability of the business or other essential terms such as access to parking. And, unfortunately, Dave failed to have an attorney review the contract. He also failed to have an accountant look at the books for the business.

As it turned out, the business had no rights to parking. Without parking, Dave had few customers and could not attract more. In addition to the money Dave paid up front for the business, he spent a great deal of money on operating the business for several months. The business was not making any profits and he soon had to close it. Dave lost everything he paid for the business, plus the initial startup money he invested.

To add insult to injury, Dave was sued by the business seller for the remainder of the payments under the contract.

The Lesson: Be sure to include all important aspects of the deal in any written contract. If it is such a good deal, then both sides should be willing to put all the important promises and representations about it in writing. Also, keep a hard copy of the contract because electronic copies may be corrupted or destroyed.

LESSON 60: "FRIENDS ARE FOREVER", BUT DON'T GO INTO BUSINESS WITH THEM

A pair of businessmen retained my services to prepare a standard commercial lease. They were friends. Bill owned land and was paying to construct a metal building that Fred, his friend, was going to lease to house his machine shop. They were both experienced in business and had already decided on the basic terms.

However, a few weeks after the lease was prepared and signed, Bill called me with a problem. It seemed that he had expected Fred, the tenant, to remain in the building for at least 10 years, but now Fred was claiming he could and would leave in two years.

I explained that the lease term they agreed upon was in fact written as two years. He said he understood that but he expected his friend to stay much longer so he could be assured of repaying the loan he received to finance the building. I had not been told of this understanding prior to drafting the contract. Consequently, I had to explain that he should have put that expectation in the contract and not relied upon his understanding of his tenant's plans, even if the tenant was a friend.

The Lesson: This case demonstrates why it is dangerous to go into business with friends. Friends tend to overlook important details, especially those relating to money. But when loss of money becomes a real possibility, a business partner often puts his economic concerns ahead of the friendship.

LESSON 61: WATCH OUT FOR THE SMALL PRINT

Samuel owned a small trucking company and was persuaded by a salesman to sign up for uniform rental services. These services included a regular pick-up of his employees' dirty uniforms and a drop-off of laundered uniforms. Samuel's wife, who functioned as his personal secretary, signed the paperwork. She indicated "Secretary" where the form contract called for a title, even though she was not the official Secretary of the corporation. The contract was typical in that it was almost completely skewed in the favor of the rental company, and it had a term of five years.

After a year or two, Samuel became dissatisfied with the quality of the uniforms that were being supplied to him, so he discussed the problem with the salesman. The salesman convinced Samuel to prepare a written letter that claimed he was satisfied with the service but simply wished to discontinue using it. Samuel simply wrote the letter as a favor to the salesman.

What he failed to realize was that the form contract contained a clause that required a dissatisfied customer to send a written letter that explained his complaints or the customer could not cancel the contract for the reason that the quality of the uniforms or service was not acceptable.

Samuel later tried to cancel the contract on those very grounds. The uniform rental company insisted that the contract continue.

Samuel stopped making the monthly payment he had agreed to in the contract and was sued for the full amount of the remaining payments that the rental company was entitled to under the terms of the contract.

Samuel had a weak case because the uniform company could easily argue that the contract was validly signed by someone with apparent authority. Almost all corporations, and even many unincorporated companies, have an officer called a "Secretary." My client's argument that the company Secretary didn't have authority to sign the contract was weak, especially since the company had ratified the contract by accepting the uniforms and paying the contractual monthly payment for over a year.

The Lesson: *Read a contract before you sign it and when you are considering cancelling it, and don't expect to get out of a written contract on a technicality.*

FINAL WORDS OF AWARENESS

There certainly is a difference between being prudent and being paranoid. But remember, a little paranoia may not be misplaced; someone really may be out to get you. In other words, you will rarely regret being cautious in evaluating the legal side of any problem, but you will probably regret being careless. As the old saying goes, "The devil is in the details". So take the time now to go over the details, and you will save all the time of dealing with a legal snafu later.

If you want to avoid legal land mines, be careful with whom you go into business, and be careful how you exit a business. Read any contract before you sign it, and make sure it includes your entire agreement. Understand what insurance you need and get it. Carefully research any real estate you are considering buying and make sure it is titled properly.

In addition, learn the basics of our courts and legal system. Buy a legal dictionary and keep copies of all financial documents. And refuse to give statements without first checking with your lawyer. Only by keeping your eyes open and your mind alert will you avoid a legal minefield.

APPENDIX A
CHOOSING A LAWYER

The best lawyer I ever knew, Ernest J. Howard, said, "Don't buy your legal services the same way you buy your toilet paper". What he was referring to were lawyers who advertise on television. While lawyer advertising may seem distasteful to some people, it is here to stay. However, do not simply pick the lawyer who has the most impressive advertisement. It's advisable to do some research instead.

Ernest J. Howard also used to say, "When you need an operation, you don't try to do it yourself, you go to a professional, a surgeon". When you have a legal problem, you should do the same thing: "go to a professional".

Lawyers, like other professionals, come in all shapes and sizes. There are general practitioners and there are specialists, just as in the medical profession. Also, as in the medical world, a good general practitioner will know when to call in, or send you to, a specialist. In general, a practicing attorney has a good working knowledge of what other local attorneys' abilities are. For example, an attorney will know who is good at a specialty like labor law and who is good at estate planning, which is why you should cultivate a good relationship with a general practitioner. Your attorney will be invaluable at referring you to a specialist, if and when you need such a referral. On the other hand, there are many legal problems that are easily and efficiently handled by a general practitioner.

One of the biggest and most important variables in legal representation is motivation. No matter how bright and experienced an attorney is, if his heart is not in a case, he will not likely to do a good job. Conversely, the annals of legal history are filled with examples of highly motivated but inexperienced attorneys winning big, important cases.

Of course, the ideal lawyer is one who is motivated to help you and intelligent and experienced enough to know the best way to do so. But remember that no matter the talents, energy, or experience of the attorney, if the facts and law are against him or her, the case will likely be lost.

In addition, because legal cases can often drag on for years, you must be able to tolerate your lawyer's personality. No matter what, an attorney is human and has his own quirks. You will have to divulge personal information to your lawyer if you want him to fully understand your case. And to a lesser or greater extent, you will have to rely on your attorney's judgment. So choose someone with whom you are comfortable and able to communicate. Don't be shy about investigating your potential legal representative before you retain him or her. Here are some questions you may want answered:

1. How long ago did you graduate from law school?

2. What legal experience have you had since then?

3. What is your experience with my particular type of case?

4. How much experience do you have at jury trials? In what courts?

5. Tell me about the last case you tried before a jury.

6. Do you consider yourself a specialist? If so, in what area or field?

7. What special training or education have you had in that area?

8. What type of work comprises the majority of your practice?

9. How will your fees be calculated? Will there be separate charges for your paralegal's time?

10. What are the primary costs you anticipate that I will incur?

If you have a weak case or a case that involves a small amount of money or if your ability to pay is severely limited and your case is not going to produce a fund out of which your attorney can be paid, your choices of attorneys will be limited.

Additionally, if you are unable to afford to hire an attorney and don't have a contingency fee type of case, you can often obtain representation from a legal services corporation attorney or a *pro bono* (serving at no cost to the client) attorney. A legal services corporation is an organization, which usually gets some government funding and some private charitable funding, with the purpose of providing free or low-priced representation to indigent clients. Unfortunately, the federal budget cutbacks of the 1980s and '90s have severely limited the legal services corporations' ability to represent indigent people, and their attorneys are very selective in what cases they will take.

Most state lawyers' groups (called Bar Associations) have programs that match indigent clients with attorneys who will represent them *pro bono* .

APPENDIX B

UNDERSTANDING ATTORNEYS' FEES

There are three basic types of attorneys' fees that typically are charged for professional legal services:

1. Hourly fees

2. Set fees

3. Contingency fees

An hourly fee is just what it sounds like, a fee charged for services performed, measured at an hourly rate. Hourly rates vary by type of legal services provided, skill and reputation of the attorney, and region. Rates generally range from $75 per hour up to $400 per hour (the higher rates are normally charged in the larger urban areas).

A set fee is a total fee quoted for the entire representation. It may be paid all at once up-front or, if the attorney agrees, in partial payments over time. Criminal case fees are generally paid up front in one payment. Occasionally, criminal fees may be stretched out over several months, but for obvious reasons, a criminal case client is usually required to finish paying his or her fees before the attorney will appear in court on the case. The attorney knows that a client who is incarcerated is highly unlikely to finish paying his fees, and the attorney would have a difficult time enforcing collection as well.

A contingency fee is one in which the payment is contingent upon the attorney making a successful recovery of money damages. Contingency fees are most commonly used in personal injury cases. While the percentage varies, the standard contingency fee is one-third of the recovery.

Typically, the attorney also advances costs in a contingency-fee case that are later subtracted from the proceeds recovered.

A retainer is simply a deposit of hourly fees that an attorney typically receives from the client and deposits in his trust account and then periodically withdraws payment of his fees from as he earns them. In years past, some attorneys would charge non-refundable retainer fees, but the modern trend is for retainer fees to be refundable.

People involved in legal disputes often want to make the opposing side pay their attorney's fees. However, the general rule is that each party must pay its own attorney's fees. The exception to this rule is where a contract or statute provides for it; for example, when a judge awards the winning side in a domestic case attorney's fees from the losing side.

Large businesses usually include an attorney's fees provision in their contracts. For example, banks and financing companies typically include a provision in their contracts that allows them to recover attorney's fees for having to pursue collection of the loans. Many of the statutes that give wronged parties the right to sue for civil damages will also provide for recovery of attorneys' fees. For example, most consumers'-rights statutes allow wronged consumers to recover attorneys' fees if they prevail.

You should have any fee agreements with an attorney in writing. If you are being charged at an hourly rate, then you should request regular statements of your account so you are not surprised at the end of your case by a large bill. Ultimately, what everyone should want is to get competent representation for a fair fee. Neither party should receive a benefit it is not entitled to receive.

APPENDIX C
WILL I WIN MY CASE?

If you file a lawsuit, then you have the **burden of proof**. That means you must present enough testimony in court to convince the jury or judge that you should win. Exactly what you have to prove varies with the type of case. In a **negligence** case you must prove three points to win your case: (1) an injury, (2) that it was directly or proximately caused by the other side's conduct, and (3) that conduct causing the injury was negligent (wrongful).

In a civil lawsuit, the definition of wrongful conduct is different than that in a criminal case. Conduct is wrongful in a civil case if it constitutes a breach of duty owed to someone else. In other words, conduct is wrongful if it invades another's rights.

One type of wrongful conduct is what is known as "negligence." Negligence is often called carelessness. For example, a careless automobile driver who runs through a stop sign or red light is guilty of negligence because he breached the duty to stop. If that breach causes an injury to another, then he will be liable to that victim for damages.

The burden of proof is often said to be higher or heavier in a criminal case than in a civil case. In a criminal case, the prosecution must prove its case **beyond a reasonable doubt**. However, in a civil case, the side bringing the suit to court (the plaintiff) must prove its case by the greater weight of the evidence (also called the **preponderance of the evidence**). The plaintiff's case must be more convincing than the other side's case. This is considered a lower burden of proof.

Regardless of the burden of proof, you must persuade the jury to believe that you should win. If the jury doesn't like you or your claim for some reason, you will lose. Generally, jurors don't like lawsuits that seem unfair or frivolous. Jurors also tend to dislike people who seem to be getting something for nothing or who seem to be making a mountain out of a mole hill.

To win your case in court, you must have incurred significant damages. You are not going to win if you do not seem to be damaged or injured in any way and if you are unable to prove that the other side is responsible for your losses.

You should discuss your case in detail with your lawyer before you have him or her file a lawsuit for you. Talk about what you will be required to prove in order to win; how likely you are to win; how much in damages you are likely to win; what costs you will incur trying to win; what problems you face in proving your case; what evidence you will need to present in court; what witnesses you will use and how your lawsuit will proceed from start to finish.

No one can predict what a jury is going to do on any particular case. A jury trial is hard work. It causes stress on all involved and can be very time consuming. Don't file for a jury trial unless you are certain you are willing to pay the costs, both financially and emotionally.

APPENDIX D
HOW NEVER TO LOSE AGAIN

This is the Introduction to my book, *Never Lose Again*, to be published soon. Please contact me or go to www.joelyles.com for more information on ordering your own copy of this valuable resource.

> *Blessed are the peacemakers….*
>
> Matthew 5:9

Everybody loves a winner. At least that is what popular culture would have us believe. Tiger Woods…Michael Jordan…Julia Roberts…Donald Trump… Warren Buffet…Oprah Winfrey…Bill Gates. The media loves these winners. Judging by the amount of media coverage these superstars receive, you would think that the rest of the world is made of worthless losers.

But what about the losers? Where is the media coverage for losers? We don't want to hear about them. It's not that we don't sympathize with losers, it's just that the stories about losers don't hold our attention. (Pat Conroy makes this point in his recent autobiographical book, *My Losing Season*.)

Young people are indoctrinated to believe that they should strive hard to win and that they should not compromise. History books are filled with battles won, but rarely mention battles avoided. Quiet compromises that move a country forward, peacefully, are quickly forgotten.

It seems that compromise is a dirty word in America. Although it should be if you are talking about compromising your ethics, here I am talking about compromising in conflicts, businesses or gambles. Most of us accept, although begrudgingly, that compromise is a key part of the political process; that legislation which passes and becomes law is the result of compromise between competing factions. But few people realize that compromise is the reality of life and is the vital oil that keeps the wheels of our civilization turning. Without compromise our government, businesses, commerce, healthcare system and educational institutions would grind to a halt. Without compromise friends would fight, spouses would divorce, families would disintegrate and even armies would fall into chaos. Why? Because compromise leads to agreement and people working together accomplish much more than people working at odds with one another.

Of course, every agreement is preceded by negotiations. If you properly prepare for those negotiations you will get most of what you want from them. The art of negotiating is explained in many books (see Appendix G); however, this book will show you not only how, but also why and when, you should negotiate compromises.

The key to never losing is to plan for a compromise that gets you what you want most, whether it is a sale, a job, a monetary settlement or just a weekend away from the house. With proper planning you can develop a strategy that allows you to "give in" on issues that are not as important as your primary goal. With this strategy of negotiating over things you are willing to trade away, you can enter the negotiation process with confidence.

There is a vast number of books, articles, seminars, and videos on how to be a winner. They will tell you how to win at investment, gambling, chess, business, sports, romance and just about any other endeavor. This book is for those who are wise enough to want to avoid losing. This book is about the value of compromise; not compromise in matters of integrity, but compromise in matters of conflict or chance. You will learn how never to lose again, even if you compromise. So read on and prepare never to lose again.

APPENDIX E
LAW DICTIONARY

Many people realize that certain words used in a legal context may mean something different than they would in everyday usage. However, few realize how important it is to understand legal terms when they are used in a contract or other documents that affect their rights, duties, and legal interests.

I strongly suggest that everyone purchase a dictionary of legal terms or use one at a library or on the Internet. Such a reference defines every legal term you are likely to encounter and also provides quotes from cases that help explain the legal context of the words.

Examples of words that have different everyday usage meanings and legal definitions include:

- Assault — Normal usage: a violent attack, either physical or verbal. Legal definition: an unlawful **attempt** or **threat** to injure another physically.

- Binder — Normal usage: A notebook cover with rings or clamps for holding sheets of paper. Legal definition: A **payment** or **written agreement** legally binding the parties to an agreement until the completion of a formal written contract.

- Complaint — Normal usage: An expression of pain, dissatisfaction, or resentment. Legal definition: The **written document** filed by the plaintiff in a civil action, setting forth the claim on which relief is sought.

- Battery — Normal usage: A device for storing electric current energy. Legal definition: The unlawful use of force to **injure** another person.

Do you find after looking over these examples that your understanding of these terms has changed a little, or a lot? If so, you have the perfect illustration of my point that using a law dictionary can be critical to safe passage through a legal minefield.

APPENDIX F
REFERENCES TO ORGANIZATIONS
SOURCES OF LEGAL INFORMATION

SOUTH CAROLINA:

South Carolina Bar
950 Taylor St.
Columbia, SC 29202
Tel: (803) 799-6653
Fax: (803) 799-4118

South Carolina Centers for Equal Justice
P.O. Box 10706 FS
Greenville, SC 29603
www.sccej.org

NORTH CAROLINA:

North Carolina Bar Association
8000 Weston Parkway
Cary, NC 27513
Tel: (919) 677-0561
Fax: (919) 677-0761

Please be aware that all states have bar associations, legal aid organizations, consumer organizations and other sources of legal assistance. Most law schools also have clinic programs which offer free legal advice and representation to the public.

NATIONAL:

National Consumer Law Centers, Inc.
77 Summer Street, 10th Floor
Boston, MA 02110-1006
Phone: (617) 542-9595
Email: www.consumerlaw.org

Earthjustice
426 17th St., 6th Floor
Oakland, CA 94612-2820
Tel: (510) 550-6700
Fax: (510) 550-6740
Email: info@earthjustice.org

Environmental Law Institute
1616 P St. NW Suite 200
Washington, DC 20036
Tel: (202) 939-3800
Fax: (202) 939.3868
Email: Law@ELI.org

Association of Trial Lawyers of America
The Leonard M. Ring Law Center
1050 31st St. NW
Washington, DC 20007-4499
Tel: (800) 424-2725 or (202) 965-3500
www.atla.org

APPENDIX G
REFERENCES TO WEBSITES AND PUBLICATIONS

WEBSITES

American Bar Association - www.abanet.org.
Choose the "General Public Resources" tab.

Association of Trial Lawyers of America -
www.atla.org. Choose the "Consumer and Media Resources" tab.

State Bar Associations - Use your preferred search engine and search using the format "South Carolina (or appropriate other state) Bar Association". The South Carolina Bar Association website is: www.scbar.org.

Federal agency clearinghouse website - www.firstgov.gov. This site has links to specific sites throughout United States and states' governments.

Most state legal aid organizations also have websites.

WEBSITES TARGETING ABUSE

www.drirene.com - Resources for abuse victims.

www.safe4all.org - Help for male victims of abuse

www.drjoecarver.com - Articles and links on abusive relationships.

PUBLICATIONS

Black's Law Dictionary, Bryan A. Garner (Ed.), 2001, West Information Pub. Group

Controlling People, Patricia Evans, 2002, Adams Media Corporation

Getting to Yes, Fisher, Ury, Patton, 1991, Penguin USA

The Verbally Abusive Relationship, Patricia Evans, 1996, Adams Media Corporation

How to Argue and Win Every Time: at Home, at Work, in Court, Every Where, Every Day, Gerry L. Spence, 1996, St. Martin's Press

The Emotionally Abusive Relationship, Beverly Engel, 2002, John Wiley & Sons, Inc.

The Intelligent Negotiator, Charles B. Craver, 2002, Prima Lifestyle

About the Author

Joseph Lyles is a practicing attorney, writer and public speaker in Greenville, South Carolina. He has represented a broad spectrum of clients on diverse cases since he was admitted to practice in 1983.

Born and raised in the small historic town of Winnsboro, South Carolina, Lyles attended Furman University in Greenville, South Carolina for two years and then transferred to Western Washington University in Bellingham, Washington, where he graduated with honors and a Bachelor of Science Degree in Environmental Studies.

After working at a variety of jobs for a year, Lyles attended the University of South Carolina, School of Law and graduated in 1983 with a Juris Doctorate degree. He was admitted to the practice of law by the South Carolina Supreme Court in November of 1983.

Lyles' first job out of law school was as a law clerk to the Honorable C. Victor Pyle, Jr., Judge of the Thirteenth Judicial Circuit in Greenville, South Carolina. He then served three years active duty in the Judge Advocate General's Corps as a military lawyer, or a JAG, in the U.S. Navy. While serving as a JAG officer, he prosecuted and defended court martials (criminal trials of service members). As a JAG, Lyles also represented service members in Administrative Boards, advised them on legal problems, and wrote Wills and Powers of Attorney. He further acted as a Special Assistant United States Attorney and acted as a Special Assistant United States Attorney and prosecuted civilians for legal violations on the military base.

As a civilian lawyer, Lyles has handled a wide variety of cases, including ones involving personal injuries; wrongful deaths; environmental issues; estate problems; contracts; divorces; custody disputes; insurance claims; conservatorships; Social Security disability claims; criminal charges; business matters; E.R.I.S.A. issues; and administrative law cases in every type of trial court in South Carolina, including Federal District Court. Additionally, he has successfully handled appeals in the state appellate courts.

Lyles lives with his family in Greenville, South Carolina. He enjoys kayaking and other outdoor sports, parenting, gardening, reading, writing, charity work, and public speaking.

Joseph Lyles may be reached at Post Office Box 17736, Greenville, South Carolina 29606, Phone (864) 294-9196 or (864) 325-2660, or by e-mail at jslyles@bellsouth.net or jslyles@aol.com. Also see www.lyles-law.com.